COUNTRY LIVES REMEMBERED

BRIAN P MARTIN
EDITED BY RUTH BINNEY

COUNTRY LIVES REMEMBERED

BRIAN P MARTIN
EDITED BY RUTH BINNEY

David and Charles

DEDICATION

To the rural labourer, who has given so much but received so little. His is a greater reward.

A DAVID & CHARLES BOOK

Copyright © Brian P. Martin 1992

Introduction and additional box text copyright
© Ruth Binney, 2010

Jacket illustration by Lucy Oldfield

First published in paperback 1999
This new edition published in 2010

Brian P. Martin has asserted his right to be
identified as author of this work in accordance
with the Copyright, Designs and Patents
Act 1988.

A catalogue record for this book is available from
the British Library.

ISBN 13: 978-0-7153-3819-3
ISBN 13: 0-7153-3819-6

Printed in China by RR Donnelley for
David & Charles Brunel House Newton Abbot
Devon

David & Charles publish high quality books on
a wide range of subjects. For more great book
ideas visit: www.rubooks.co.uk

BY THE SAME AUTHOR

Tales of the Old Gamekeepers
*The Great Shoots – Britain's Premier Sporting
Estates*
Sporting Birds of Britain and Ireland
Birds of Prey of the British Isles
Tales of the Old Villagers
Tales from the Country Pub
Tales of Time & Tide
More Tales of the Old Countrymen
More Tales of the Old Gamekeepers

CONTENTS

THE THREE AGES OF COUNTRYMEN

At heart we are all countrymen;
it's just that some have lost their roots
and need reminding of days when
grandfather walked in greener boots.

In childhood nature leads life's dance
as green ways beg us to explore
and every season brings romance
but summer lasts for evermore.

In middle age we drift away
in search of gold, and more and more,
and even on our better days
see country fields as factory floor.

But in old age romance returns
to haunt the heart of yesteryear
and then the countryman soon yearns
for fields and woods he once held dear.

BRIAN P MARTIN, 1991

INTRODUCTION

I t is, perhaps, an inevitable aspect of human nature that it is only when things we take for granted are threatened with an uncertain future, or even extinction, that we really come to appreciate their true worth. This sentiment has never applied more aptly than in relation to the countryside and the men and women who still work to maintain it and make use of its resources, whether as farmers or coppicers, thatchers or beekeepers, or in dozens of other different ways.

The colourful characters you will meet in this book, whose hard working but so often entertaining lives and memories are described in vivid detail by Brian P Martin, are our link with the countryside of the relatively recent past. They highlight both the intense hardship of previous generations but also the ways in which those close to the land appreciated and worked it with respect and used its resources with care, ever mindful of the need to work with, not against nature. Nearly all have passed away or retired since their stories were first recounted, and you will see that they all experienced huge amounts of change as their lives progressed, but they spring to life from every page as examples of rural trades and occupations that remain vital to the continuance of country traditions.

As the health, well-being and future of our countryside and all it contains are increasingly threatened, so it is ever more vital to look back to the past – as through these engrossing biographies – and to the needs of the present. Yet while reflecting in such a way it is also encouraging to discover that there is a huge and continuing upsurge of interest in country pursuits and careers. Country crafts are becoming valued in a way that has not been so for a generation, and it is becoming ever easier to enrol for courses in order to train properly for in of these. To help foster this interest, brief details are included for all the occupations included in this book, along with some fascinating reflections on country life in past generations as recorded in the eras before those of the characters featured in these pages.

Anyone who loves the countryside and its people will value these tales and respect the labour of those who dedicated their lives to its service. There is so much to learn from them, not least their practicality, their connection with nature and, of course, their humour.

Ruth Binney
West Stafford, Dorset 2010

THE VOICE OF NATURE

Jim Scard
Mole-catcher and Pest Controller

When I drove into the Wiltshire village of Broad Chalke, a few miles south-west of Salisbury, I asked a paper-boy if he knew where Jim Scard lived. With a chuckle, the lad replied: 'Everyone knows that'. His reply was not surprising, for I was seeking a man whom folk of every station had been calling on for decades, seeking his help both for individuals and for the community at large. He is the countryman's countryman, whose great knowledge of rural ways and wildlife is firmly rooted in a lifetime's outdoor employment in many fields. But it is primarily in pest control that this unassuming character has made his mark.

Born in Weymouth, Dorset, on 1 March 1916, Gordon Mortimer Scard (later known to everyone as Jim) never knew his father, a baker who died while Jim was still a toddler. It was his stepfather, 'an ex-Artillery chap', who pointed him towards a country occupation. His mother was a cook.

The newly united family moved to Lavington, 5 miles south of Devizes, in Wiltshire, when Jim was nine. His earliest memories are of schooldays at Woodford, near Salisbury, which had been his home since he was 4. There were about 120 children at Woodford school – 'every village had a lot of kids because there were many more labourers on the land in those days and almost everyone had a large family'.

One of his schoolteachers was a Yorkshireman 'who was dead keen on cricket. I was only there a week when he gave me a halfpenny for catching him out, but a few days later he caned me with a little willow stick for smoking a broken clay-pipe that someone had thrown away.'

But even before he went to school Jim was attracted to the land. He often used to go out with Fred and Bill Bayford, who were carters and ploughmen and just two of 12 men who were employed on the mixed Home Farm. Jim remembers their horses – 25-30 lovely animals' – with great affection. 'There were two teams so that they could change over at lunchtime, but some men had to take an early lunch to sharpen the cutters. Harvesting was with McCormick and Albion binders and they never started till the dew was off because when the canvasses on the machines got wet the tension was spoiled.

'When the horses were set in their furrows, the ploughmen sometimes used to let them walk on a bit while they stopped to shoot starlings with a catapault. I ate one once – roasted it over a fire. Never again.

'In the summer they used to bring the young horses out. I always remember one which took over two hours to go round the field just once. Every time the old horses went forward he went back. Trouble was the youngsters were easily scared by the banging of the machinery.

'One of my earliest memories is of watching 'em lungeing – a horse going round and round a person on a long lead for hours on end to break it in. But the first chore every day was to feed and clean the lot – at 6 am.'

Wherever you went in the 1920s, horses toiled the long day across every landscape, including the fields of New Farm, on the Blandford road 2 miles from Coombe Bissett, where Jim's father worked for Ernie White. 'One day old White said, "Bring young Jim over", so I went on the Saturday to do a bit of hoeing. "You'll need something to work with", he said, so he sent me over to Phil the carter, who gave me a muck-scraper. So back I went with it to knock on White's door and said "Will this do?". "Buggers", said White. "You go back and tell 'em not to be so silly." But it was all good fun. Everyone had a laugh in those days.'

Jim helped his father with the hoeing 'for 30 bob an acre. This was flat hoeing between the rows. Three weeks later we'd clean right round each plant – mangolds, swedes, turnips.'

When Jim was 12 years old, the family went to live at New Farm. 'Father got a house there because he was available to the farmer for building work as well as haymaking and other jobs. He was a really good builder – I could show you a path now we made 60 years ago, and there's been a few thousand feet over that.'

On leaving school at 14, Jim became a labourer on New Farm. He had passed his exams to go on for further education but, like most country folk then, the family simply could not afford it.

'In those days you was a real farm labourer and did a bit of everything – rolling, harrowing, ploughing and hedge-trimming as well as helping out with the animals. By golly, I really earned my starting wage of 10s, but I did get 3d an hour overtime after fifty hours in a week, working 6 am to 5 pm.'

Jim has mixed memories of White. 'He was a cruel man. One day he went to milk a heifer and she kicked him, so he set about her with a milking stool. He used to put a strap around their legs and then push them till they fell over. After a fright like that all he had to do was tie the strap round their legs again and they wouldn't budge an inch, let alone kick him.

'Nobody ever worked on Sunday. Only the milking was done then – 30 cows twice a day by hand. Sunday afternoon was red letter – that was when we put on our clean smocks. One day Ernie was walking by in his when a cow "coughed" an' he got dung all over him, so he hit her with a milking stool. Yes, he certainly was a hard man.

'But he was a marvellous thatcher of ricks and taught me all there was to know. The secret was to start in the middle and we'd mark it out with sticks. In those days a farmer could eye up a piece of cut corn and estimate the size of the rick very accurately.'

Despite his tough exterior, White was a chapel parson. 'He used to take me down with him, but after giving the Baptists and Methodists a good try I decided on the church. Most of all, I didn't like the chapel because White used to stand around for ages afterwards, haggling with all the other farmers over this and that when I wanted to get off home.

'First thing on Mondays we cleaned out the cattle and fed them. Each cow had its own tin for the feed – cotton-cake and linseed-cake bought in. But I never minded this because straight after we went ferreting for the day – or snaring if wet – on the downs. Ernie slung all the wires around his waist and I carried the pegs and tillers. I made up the snares, handed them to Ernie and he stamped them in. We'd set about 250 in the day between milkings. White would go back on Tuesday morning and often collect about 40-50 rabbits which he'd take to market that day. In the meantime I'd be milking. In winter we set the snares Friday and picked up Saturday as the rabbits kept longer.

'When Ernie went to market the farm labourers had a good chance to play a trick on him. He used to pay them 2d a tail for moles. Every pay day the tails was tipped out onto the floor and counted. Then Ernie put 'em in a tin and took 'em to the dung heap. But as soon as he'd done the men used to fetch some of them out again so they was paid twice.

'There were lots of English partridges about then, but very few French (the red-legged) because the farmers believed they drove the native birds off, so they tried to get rid of them. There were loads of hares and foxes, too, but very few pheasants. They used to grow mustard as a manure which was ploughed in- the partridges loved it. And every spring we had wonderful carpets of wild flowers, especially violets.

'White used to sell his shooting, but there were no reared birds. A doctor and two friends took it and come harvest time they asked if they could shoot a few of the rabbits bolting out of the corn as it was cut. White said OK and told us workers to watch it – "Don't chase 'em like you usually do." And of course we didn't go much on this as the rabbits was our perks. In those days I used to throw father's old blackthorn shillelagh at rabbits and I had loads with it. So, as soon as the doctor fired the first shot old Bill fell off the binder clutching his ear. Much to our relief, White immediately said that was it – the shooting had to stop.'

Later, Jim became a keen shooter. He has been back with a team of Guns to Home Farm, where he lived as a boy, and they shot 287 hares. 'But that's nothing, we've killed 420 in a day down here in the valley. The numbers went down when they started using this Paraquat weedkiller.'

When Jim's family left New Farm to live at Allenford, near the village of Martin, he went to work for Levi Shearing as under-dairyman. Again, it was very hard work, not least because he had to spend a couple of hours a day pumping up enough water for the cattle.

'At first the rats in the granary there was terrible, so I said to Levi's sister, Francis, "Look, I'll see to them for you". 'She said she'd give me a packet of Star cigarettes, which then cost 4d for ten. But I said no, I wanted a packet of Players, which cost 1s for 20. A fortnight later she was so desperate she agreed. So Jim Woodford and me went over and we got dozens with Jim's specially sharpened spike. The poor old ferret was bitten all over. I even took a flat board and knocked 'em down as they ran up the walls.

'Francis used to pay us a penny for each duck egg we gathered up from the riverbank. And I made a bit from the rabbits there, too. Levi said I could go for them as long as we split 50-50. So I went on Boxing Day and had eight or more. A dealer came by and we stood out for 1s each. He would have sold them for about 1s 6d a time.'

After two years at Allenford, Jim went to Beaulieu as under-dairyman for a Scot called Malcolm. 'For some reason he always called me Seamus. I always remember going to the great big cauldron in his kitchen every morning to get some nice warm water to wash the cows down before milking.

'Malcolm was hit by an old Morris van down at Lepe, in the Forest. He got up, walked round the front of the vehicle and dropped dead. His son took the farm for a while but then sold up and I went to Malcolm's brother's.

'Oh, I nearly forgot; I had 12 months working at a hen battery on a bonus. When I went there the feed troughs were full of stale meal and grit and the water troughs were half full of silt washed off the hens' bills. And out back if there was one rat there was a hundred. So I said to Mr Towell, "Do you mind if I have a good cleanup?" "Not at all", he said, "I want the production up". Immediately I started three feeds a day instead of one, and believe you me the eggs shot up. We had 1,008 birds, all in cages. But there were men on the free range too. I really enjoyed it there.

'Those old hens was funny things. One day a grass snake came in and really drove 'em mad. He'd been taking the eggs, which is one of their favourite foods. I watched one eating a frog at Beaulieu once. He slimed all over it first, but what amazed me was the frog made no attempt to escape, even though the two animals were face to face and the snake's jaws widening. Afterwards, I stamped on the snake's head and out came the frog. He seemed all right.'

Despite his love of the land, Jim had always been very interested in flying and had wanted to join the Royal Air Force when he left school, but his mother would not give the necessary permission. However, when the prospect of war loomed large, the idea of joining up crossed Jim's mind again. He had been thinking about it anyway because of the awful way some farmers treated the labourers – even after a lifetime's loyal service. 'The last straw came when I went to a dance and saw my girlfriend on someone else's lap. That was it, I gave Mr Malcolm a month's notice.

'Stepfather said, "What do you want to go in?" I said, "The RAF, of course". He said, "Well, you'd better hurry before they call you up and stick you in the infantry." So I did, and in 1938 started at Uxbridge. After 58 weeks at Henlow I qualified as an electrician and was later posted to 10 Bomber Gunnery School at Warmwell.

'My daily inspection only took 30 minutes, so I got cheesed off and learnt to drive a tractor. I became a bowser driver and towed petrol out to the planes. One day I was driving the tractor down one of the very narrow lanes around the camp, which was out on the heath, when this great big car came hurtling towards me. I had no choice but to swerve off the road straight through the hedge, but it was only a bit of blackthorn and I had no worries in the tractor. Out jumped the chauffeur and said, "His Majesty is very sorry but we have to get to London in a hurry". Turned out it was the King of Norway.'

Even when he was in the RAF, Jim managed to do a spot of rabbiting – poaching really. 'Every morning at Little Stoughton in Bedfordshire in came the policeman and his chums and if there was a rabbit hanging on the door they'd have it. And sometimes there was a pheasant or two from behind the bomb dump. I got in with the local squire and he let me go on some neighbouring ground in return for repairing some old electrical equipment. He wanted me to take up a job as keeper after the war.'

Jim left the RAF as a sergeant in 1945. 'I wrote to the Post Office, but they said I would have to start at the bottom and I didn't want that. Also, I could have gone to a large electrical company, but I didn't want to travel all the way to Bournemouth every day.'

In 1940 Jim had married Violet, and his diary shows just how much he looked forward to her letters during those seemingly endless postings in the RAF. At first they lived with Violet's widowed father, but later moved into a council house at New Town, Broad Chalke. 'They had to put me top of the list', Violet told me. 'I was born and bred here – in that thatched cottage just over there. I reckon I know every field in Broad Chalke. I could go out blind and I wouldn't fall in the bank. I don't think I'd be happy anywhere else.'

Sadly now crippled by arthritis, 70-year-old Violet is the daughter of a carter, who was in charge of 30 horses. 'He was a real countryman – used to go by the clouds an' all.'

To most outsiders, Broad Chalke still appears a pretty, sleepy village where one could retire in peace, but for Violet, who has lived nowhere else, there are regrets. 'Half these houses used to be full of farm workers, but then came the tractors and they didn't want the men. After that all the weekenders came in.

'Another sad thing is how all the flower shows are disappearing. In the old days every village had one. I always used to get and do the teas, but in the end hardly anyone appreciated it; there's a funny lot of people now. Trouble is, stuff's got so dear, what with the electric required for bringing the plants on an' all.'

Not surprisingly, I sense that Violet would rather go back to those idyllic times between the wars. 'In them days we only used to see one car a week, and that was either the doctor's or the vicar's. Dad used to take two-and-a-half hours to go by cart to Salisbury and back. Now its in the car and gone – it's all too quick out in the country now.

'When we were kids we used to make tents out of the wheatsheafs. We stacked 'em up and 'ad our tea or lunch in 'em when we took dad's out to the fields. Everyone had to make their own enjoyment then. Also, every village had its own maypole and May Queen. Now we never seem to get the maypole weather. Take this year: instead of watching everyone dancin' an' having fun we was all cussin' because it was cold as charity.'

At the age of 14 Violet started to work as a housemaid for the Hussey family at 14s a week. 'They had all that heavy silver and it was my job to clean it. After five years of that I went to Beaulieu and that's where I met my husband.

'Out in the field lunch used to be the top of a cottage loaf, cheese and a hunk of butter. We also used to make rook pie with onion and egg and nice thick gravy. There was lovely lambs'-tail pie too, but you can't make 'em now because they put those rings round the tails to make 'em wither away.'

Violet's continuing love of the Wiltshire countryside was certainly influential in Jim's life after the war, but it was a fortuitous meeting which provided his next job. He was doing some decorating when he got into conversation with someone from the War Agricultural Executive Committee (WARAG). 'I was to start that Monday, in pest control, and by golly those pests had bred like mad during the war. Funny thing is, I would have to drive all over the place and the only thing I'd ever been on the road with was a tractor. But there was no driving test then.'

The rabbit was the greatest agricultural pest during the 1940s' but Jim was also concerned with rats and moles. He earned £4 10s a week, but was allowed to sell the rabbits to butchers for a bonus of 2½d for a large one and ½d for a 'tiddler'. This was certainly a great incentive because on some days he killed 150. 'With the head and legs off I used to skin 'em in 25 seconds. But it wasn't always easy to get rid of large numbers locally. Once I sold 150 a week to the local hospital, but that was all spoilt by the arrival of cheap Australian and Chinese rabbits. They're too sweet, you know, nothing like a wild one – rather like the difference in flavour between field and cultivated mushrooms.'

In his first year Jim made £1,000 profit for local farmers in controlling their rabbits. No wonder the WARAG Wiltshire committee described him as 'a man in a million'.

Jim still has the records which show how many rabbits there were after the war. But there were just as many rats, too. His record day was in January 1947 when he and his mate killed 386 rats at Ford Slaughterhouse, near Salisbury. 'We pre-baited with sausage rusk on the Monday and Tuesday, and when we went back for the kill on Wednesday the rats was queuing up for more – just like chickens. I thought, "Good God, there's more rats here than ever Mondays". I went round to where all the guts were tipped and over the back all the rat runs showed up in the frost, going right away to where they were still thrashing ricks across the field. As the ricks were done the rats were streaming over and all the animal bones were picked absolutely clean.

'We added our zinc phosphide to the rusk they was so keen on, knowing that we wouldn't have to wait long the poison causes water on the lungs and the rats more or less drown within a few minutes. But as fast as they died others kept on coming. Never seen anything like it. However, when we went back later it was quiet as a grave. We buried the rats quickly, but later we decided to dig 'em up again for a photograph.'

Since then Jim has killed many thousands of rats for many people in many different situations, but he has been bitten by one only twice. The first time was when he put his hand in a hole and pulled out three rabbits. 'I thought I had another, but it turned out to be a damn rat, which bit my finger then ran up my arm and away. So off I went to the doctor. He said, "What do you want?" I told him I needed some treatment, what with the black death an' all. But he just said, "Don't be so silly, a human bite's worse".

'The second time was when I thought I saw a rabbit's foot in a hollow tree. I thought, "I'll have you", and grabbed hold as fast as I could. There was a squeal and he bit right down through my nail and thumb.'

On another occasion Jim was bitten by a fox. One was required for a foxhunt, so Jim's expert services were called upon. Eventually, the dogs marked one to ground, but it was in a hole which had been squashed by a passing tank, so it had to lie on its side. 'Because of

A SHREWD OBSERVER

A MOLE-CATCHER, Miss Mitford has said, 'is of the earth, earthy'; but he is of the green fields, of the solitary woodlands. We observe him, especially in the spring and the autumn, a silent and picturesque object, poring under hedges and along the skirts of the forest, or the margin of a stream, for traces of the little black-a-moor pioneer Grubbing his way in darkness drear

We have met him in copses and hazel-shaded lanes, cutting springs for his traps; and we not only love him, and look upon him as one of the legitimate objects of rural scenery, but have often found him a quiet but shrewd observer of nature, and capable of enriching us with many fragments of knowledge. In the winter by the fire he makes his traps. These are very simple machines, which almost any one may construct. We have made and set many a one ourselves, and have been up by the earliest dawn of day to discover their success. Many moles may be caught in one place, if the trap be judiciously set in a main burrow. It is better near a hedge, or in a plantation, than in the middle of a field, where it is liable to be disturbed by cattle. A strong hazel stick for the spring, two pieces of brass wire, a little string; a few hooked pegs, and a top made of the half of a piece of willow pole, about 6 inches long and 3 in diameter, hollowed out, are all the requisites for a mole-trap.

WILLIAM HOWITT
Book of the Seasons, 1830

this I had to grab him by the side of the neck instead of the back. My mate said, "He's going to bite you", and with that the bugger screwed his head round and bit my arm. Well, my fingers stood right out and I dropped him immediately, but I managed to catch him between my knees and without further fuss we popped him in the sack. Funny thing is, after all that bother, when he was released some miles away he managed to run all the way back home.'

Very many years later, Jim could still take you to where this and many other little incidents happened. For example, there was the time in about 1950, when he put down good hay for the rabbits in deep snow. 'Would you believe it, they ignored it and preferred to dig down for roots. But I still know exactly where that was because the seed from the hay rooted and you can still recognise the patch.'

Rabbits were very much Jim's main source of income for many years. After working for WARAG, he went into partnership with the man who used to buy most of his catch. 'C.A. (Dick) Nunn was a real character, Jimmy Edwards' double, and we employed 11 trappers.' During that time Jim and a lad once caught 2,040 rabbits in one week, 425 of them on a single day. 'That was my best ever and I put it down to the snow. They knew it was coming all right and was all out and about to fill their bellies – that's when we caught 'em.'

Such quantities of rabbits could not all be disposed of locally so Dick and Jim used to take them up to Smithfield Market, in London. 'The first time I went there I had about 250 aboard the one-tonner and as soon as I arrived I started to unload 'em. But that was the worst thing I could have done – I was breaking the rules and the porters wouldn't touch them; they were a rough old lot. So I had

to drive all the way back with 'em, and it was a long old drag up there then.'

But those days of rabbit superabundance were not to last; with the introduction of myxomatosis in the early 1950s the population was almost wiped out, and with it went Jim's living. But ever resourceful, he immediately rang six farmers in the district and was promised six contracts for rat extermination, worth £160 per annum – 'not bad in those days.

'My partner went off and bought a pig farm. He was a real nutcase. Once he blew up some badgers with a tubful of carbide. Unfortunately, the fuse went out so he took back a turf at the sett, stepped back and fired his Very pistol into the hole. My God, there was such an almighty explosion he singed his eyebrows and he half-disappeared when all the ground around him collapsed. He never did see any of the badgers. But they really did play havoc with the rabbits.

'After that I started to get my own rabbit-control contracts as well. At one time I had 90,000 acres, including Porton Down, where the Government had their biological research establishment. Some of the areas up there were fenced in – and still are – but I always thought it funny that the rabbits could wander in and out of some no-go areas even though they could catch anthrax and everything.'

Apart from rabbits and rats, Jim's pest-control work has also involved a variety of 'bugs'. Among his most memorable experiences was when he was called to Wroughton Hospital, at Swindon, to deal with an infestation of cockroaches. 'I started in the morning in number 1 kitchen, and when I got to the top – number 19 kitchen – in the afternoon the cook there said: "I knew you were coming at 10 am because they were coming up the pipes in troops".'

On another cockroach occasion Jim went to the officers' mess at Old Sarum. 'I walked the kitchen at night when all was quiet and followed 'em back to base like a regiment of ants. There were masses of 'em and I tracked 'em down to a crockery store, where I sprayed with Lindane pyrethrum, which lasts for about three months. The kitchen staff used to sweep up the bodies by the shovelful.'

Over many summers Jim has dealt with hundreds of wasps' nests, but has only ever been stung twice. Like all good pest controllers he will not kill bees, but he has been called to move them on. 'The best way is to put old oil or strong disinfectant underneath them – that's usually enough.'

In carrying out his work Jim has rarely been questioned. But one incident brought a smile to his face as he told me about it. 'I used to do regular work for Lady Essex. One day she asked me how it was that I kept going there to put poison down but they never saw any rats. So I was really cross and said, "OK, I'll see to that". When I next had a load of bodies I put 'em in a sack and took 'em to her door. When she was summoned I tipped 'em out all over the ground. She screamed and was gone. I was never questioned again.

'Some fifteen years later, I offered to cut her grass, but she was divorced and struggling then, so she said only if the price was right. I remember it well, because afterwards she gave me tea and it was so awful I had to pour it into a flower pot when she wasn't looking. She

THE PET TOAD

I HAVE been informed, from undoubted authority, that some ladies took a fancy to a toad, which they nourished summer after summer, with the maggots which turn to flesh flies. The reptile used to come forth every evening from an hole under the garden-steps; and was taken up, after supper, on the table to be fed.

But at last a tame raven gave him such a severe stroke with his horny beak as put out one eye. After this accident the creature languished for some time and died.

GILBERT WHITE
Natural History and Antiquities of Selborne, 1789

really was a strange person – used to wander around barefoot in the nettles collecting apples.'

But even if they were eccentric, few people would ever dare to question Jim's knowledge of moles. During a lifetime's trapping he has found their numbers to be surprisingly steady, with only little ups and downs and no clear trends. 'But strangely, on some days almost entirely bucks or bitches are caught.'

In recent years, Jim has received between 10p and 20p each for mole-skins, but moles are rarely caught just for their skins. Jim is paid by the hour or by contract and, operating alone, he can easily undercut the often excessive fees of big pest-control firms, yet still make a good living.

Jim started to trap before World War II and has been called upon to clear some pieces of ground many times over. As I walked with him along the River Avon in the Woodford Valley, on Lord Chichester's estate, he told me: 'If I wiped out every mole here others would come back through the same runs within ten years'.

Although he also deals with infestations in public playing-fields and gardens, Jim works mainly for farmers. The mole is unwanted by them for a variety of reasons: by tunnelling beneath seed-drill lines in search of the insect larvae that attack seeds, subsequent wilting and destruction of young plants may result; the mole-hills cover valuable pasture or hay; it throws up stones which may damage valuable cutting machinery; soil fouling silage may lead to harmful fermentation, and mole-hills serve as seed-beds for vigorous colonising weeds. On the other hand, the mole's effect on worm numbers is not thought to be significant and its deep tunnelling in damp ground probably improves the drainage.

On the thin soil of the chalk hills around Salisbury, the shallow mole runs are readily detected and the galvanised spring traps are easily set in them. 'I wouldn't hang up a new one, but bury it in the soil ready for use', Jim told me, referring to the mole's sense of smell. 'And after you set each trap you must carefully replace the turf or soil over it, for if they see the light they will bung up the run and not use it.'

It is easy to see if a trap has been sprung because the spring pokes through the earth. As we checked a line, Jim said: 'Look, this old trap is sprung but there is nothing in there as it is open to the full extent'. It was an old open-ended trap that Jim had dug up over 40 years ago and he believes it to be over 100 years old. 'They've lost the art of making them now.'

Over the years, Jim has trapped by accident 'many voles, a few weasels, one grass snake and a woppin' great lobworm'. Replacing a trap, he paused to tell me how important it is to press down the bottom of the run again to make it as shiny as it is when the moles run up and down. 'They travel a tidy old distance in a day, but they always go back to a bank where it is drier.'

I asked Jim if it is essential to wear gloves to avoid leaving human scent. 'Well … yes, but it's mainly to keep the dirt off', he said with a grin. Then he cursed for he had forgotten to bring up a mole from

another colony to mix the scent. 'They don't like that – soon smell 'e and get in my trap.' In fact, each animal is usually the sole occupant of a tunnel system, but there is some sharing with subordinates coming out when the dominant mole is at rest.

Moles are active day and night, with periods of almost continuous activity lasting some 4½ hours, alternating with periods of about 3½ hours rest in the nest. Jim has found them to be 'specially active one hour after dawn, at midday and teatime'. There is slightly more activity during daylight.

We moved on steadily with Jim's arthritic knee becoming rather troublesome on a very steep hill over which late snow-clouds swooped but passed intact. With 20 miles to walk on a long day, going around the traps six times when they are working well, and mostly seven days a week between November and March, Jim is indeed a dedicated character. With 50 traps he will catch about 60 moles in 20 hours work.

Jim also poisons moles with strychnine, which he obtains from a chemist, but only under licence from the Ministry of Agriculture. Furthermore, the poison must not be used on non-agricultural land without prior approval of the Ministry's divisional executive officer. Given the choice, Jim would always use poison in preference to traps whenever he can get the bait worms – he uses 10-121b in one day! The worms are soaked in a strychnine solution for at least six hours and then two or three are dropped at suitable points in the runs, which are detected with a moling bar. Here the use of tweezers and gloves is essential. Afterwards, each hole is carefully blocked over with a small stone and the turf and earth replaced. That is the end of it. The poisoned moles are never recovered.

I tackled Jim about secondary poisoning in the food chain. He assured me: 'In 60 years poisoning I have never found a poisoned mole on top of the ground and I have never had a fatality involving another wild creature or domesticated animal or bird. However, moles are cannibalistic and it is not unusual for one to eat the body of another that has been poisoned.'

Jim has found that strychnine will kill a healthy mole within a minute, but is even quicker if the animal has a cut on its mouth. He emphasises the importance of giving enough bait, for he would hate to think of a part-poisoned mole. Any poisoned worms not eaten simply dissolve into the ground after about forty-eight hours.

Between April and October Jim traps only at weekends, for then he concentrates on gardening jobs, which is just as well because the moles go deeper in the drier months and the winter skins are the best. There are three moults – one in the spring, with the males almost a month later than the females; a second between July and September (which may not be completed), and a third between October and December. These are concurrent in all age groups and both sexes. Jim told me that 'when they shed their winter fur it can be plucked quite easily'. One strange phenomenon that he has noticed but does not know the reason for is that 'The buck often has the fur pulled out of his chest when caught in the mating season'. Perhaps this is the result of males fighting.

'The skins should be removed and pegged out within twelve hours and stretched to 4 × 5in or 4½ × 4½in.'

You can delve into the most authoritative textbooks for a host of mole facts and figures, but only long and acute observation by a true countryman such as Jim will yield those fascinating extra comments such as 'the little bitches do all the work' and 'you often find a main run where they come down to drink. A river is no barrier, for not only will the mole tunnel under the river bed, but also it is a good swimmer, using all four limbs.

'See the roots growing up through this heap', said Jim. 'This is an old, stale run and it is not worth setting a trap here.' The deeper runs obviously need more careful detection and, apart from some which had been trodden in by livestock, I simply could not see what Jim could, through the discerning eyes of experience.

Without pausing in his labours, Jim besieged me with a variety of further information about moles and other wildlife such as: 'A fox will dig out a dead mole and roll on 'im you know.' Actually, the mole is not a great source of food for predators, but during the dispersal of young from the nest, the tawny owl and other birds of prey account for many.

After mating between March and May, the mole usually has one litter of three or four in May or June, but Jim has occasionally recorded five. Although the sex ratio is approximately 1:1, 'the males are generally more trappable and particularly in the breeding season when they may outnumber the females by 3:1 in a trapping catch'.

Although it was still early in the year, Jim was able to show me a few of the larger nursery mounds, which are also known as fortresses. These are of a more permanent nature and are likely to occur where there is a bad infestation, which Jim believes 'is best dealt with quickly by laying traps or poison around the perimeter of the field'.

It is strange how some people begin to behave and almost look like their pets and favourite animals, yet Jim Scard certainly does not remind me of a mole. However, in watching him operate it almost seems that he has acquired some of the mole's amazing detection methods. While the mole's hearing and smell are only moderate and its eyes barely functional, it does have highly developed tactile sense organs that help to locate worms which, Jim assures me, 'they clean with their front limbs as they eat them'. Short vibrissae on the muzzle are associated with specialised sensory receptors and hairs on the tail tip are also sensory. The tail is carried vertically.

But despite his preoccupation with moles and other pests, Jim has always found time to develop other interests. One of his great loves is singing. 'I first sang in a choir at Martin village, where the old schoolmaster taught me to harmonise, and at school I was always called on to sing the first verse of every hymn. I used to do a duet with a girl, but she couldn't bear to face the class so she turned to the wall while I faced the others.'

Nowadays Jim still sings in the choir at Bower Chalke and Broad Chalke and is one of the 45 Bower Chalke Valley Singers, run by Mrs Hornby, wife of ex-Halifax Building Society chairman Richard Hornby, who lives at Bower Chalke in the house where William Golding – author of *Lord of the Flies* and other novels – used to live. Jim told me: 'Bill Golding became very successful rather late in life and always wanted everything instant, so when he decided he wanted two oaks for the garden it was not surprising that he wanted big ones. No acorns for him. He ordered

them from Hillier's and I had to dig the holes – 6ft deep and
4ft across!

'I was there all day. Eventually Bill came out and asked how things
were going. I said all right, but I'd better go soon as the moon was
coming out. He said, "You'd better have some cool refreshment", so
he disappeared into the house and soon came back with a great big
tumbler of whisky – and then another. With that inside me I just kept
on digging and ended up so deep I couldn't get out. Luckily, my wife
rang up to find out where I was and Bill came out to find out what's
what. Laugh … he had to fetch me a short ladder. I couldn't get out
anyway because I was just about legless. Goodness knows how I
managed to get home!'

Gardening has always played a very important part in the lives of
Jim and Violet Scard, both professionally and for recreation. Even
now Jim refuses to let the grass grow under his feet and any time you
call he is likely to be out tending his plot or someone else's. 'Just look
at this soil', he said to me on a recent visit. 'Dry as a chip already and
there's certain to be another hosepipe ban.'

Among Jim's multitude of cups and certificates for prize-winning
vegetables and flowers are a number for leeks, the growing of which
he takes very seriously. 'Always make sure the earth is a quarter inch
below the bottom two leaves. 'Always keep hoeing – just tickling up
– and always keep the white covered. Also, try to avoid watering 'em
from the top. It's disastrous if the water only goes halfway down as
then the roots start to come up to reach the water. If you must water,
then make sure you give a good drowning.'

Despite the rivalry, Jim has managed to retain a keen sense of
humour about the vegetable plot. 'Not so long ago a local newspaper

reporter came out to see me and said, "I hear you're the leek grower; I suppose you'll never be beaten". I said I dare say I will, but when he came to write it up he put that I said I would never be beaten. Do you know, in the very next show I only got second, yet there was no doubting my leeks was best. I suppose when they all saw the newspaper report they got together and said we'll stop his bragging.'

Jim's interest in gardening has resulted in his being co-opted onto the local flower show committee (for which he was chairman for ten years). 'In any village if you do something you soon get known and roped in. Before I knew it, I was secretary and then chairman of the parish council. But the council doesn't have much real power you know. I packed it in about ten years ago. Oh yes, I was also secretary of the hall committee for two years.' And as if all this wasn't enough, Jim managed to do 26 years voluntary service for the Royal Observer Corps, 'first plotting aircraft and later fall-out – all simulated of course'.

Now in his late seventies, Jim is supposed to be winding down, but he is a restless soul and his remains a working house, with few frills inside. It's as if all the love has gone on the garden. Inside, heaps of old accounts and other papers and bits and pieces burst from every drawer and adorn every ledge. The couple have six daughters and a son, but they are now all grown up and setting roots in other parts of the country. Yet young Jim is following in his father's footsteps and already giving the moles and rabbits of Wiltshire a tough time.

Nowadays, pinned down by the scourge of arthritis, Violet Scard spends much of her time sitting quietly by a coal fire. But she is never alone. A cockatiel calls incessantly from a large cage in the corner and only feet from the window finches, tits and nuthatches come for the food which Jim constantly supplies. It is a fitting place to reflect on village and country life. 'When we first came to this house we used to lie in bed at four in the morning and listen to a tremendous sound from all the songbirds. Now it's a bit different – there just aren't the numbers. But you can always bet that a cuckoo

Molehills everywhere from lawns to graveyards are a continuing annoyance, and now the use of strychnine has been banned, trapping remains the only realistic option for dealing with them. Traditionalists still favour the barrel trap method of mole catching, although the barrels are now usually made of metal rather than wood. Experts prefer these, or scissor-style traps, rather than sonic devices which serve only to repel moles and induce them to move from one site to another. To find a trained molecatcher in your area – or to find out how to become one – click onto www.britishmolecatchers.co.uk. Gardeners remain even less enamoured of rabbits, which can decimate vegetable crops in a matter of hours. Rather than killing them, rabbit-proof fencing has become the preferred method of control, although in the country the gun and ferret will still do the job in the age-old way.

Rats, too, are a continuing menace all over Britain, especially in cities. According to a recent report, there are an estimated 80 million brown rats (Rattus norvegicus) in the UK, making an average of some 1.3 rats per person, up by 39 per cent since 2000. And, thanks to council cuts in bin collections, poor sewage maintenance and flooding, their numbers are rising. There are many ways of catching rats, varying from traps to poisons, but to be effective, extermination remains a job for the expert rather than the amateur. The British Pest Control Association (www.bpca.org.uk) is an excellent source of information and training on all aspects of controlling pests safely, efficiently and within the law.

will come here on 19 April. Then he'll be quiet for a few days before you hear him again.'

Despite their years and life of hardship, Jim and Violet remain a cheerful and active couple. Jim still swings his old Volvo estate about the narrow lanes with all the quick-wittedness of that young tractor driver who once swerved to miss the King of Norway. In the front garden is the hulk of another Volvo estate, which burnt out when he was doing topiary work for pop star Toyah Wilcox. 'The tailgate light shorted and the fire gutted the back of the car. But the engine was still running so we brought it back here and I've been using it for spares as well as a store.' How typical of Jim that nothing should go to waste.

Sadly, Jim Scard died in August 1995.

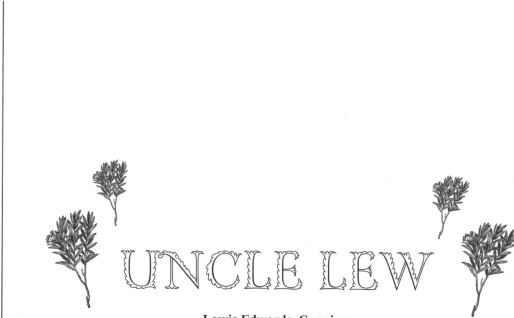

UNCLE LEW

Lewis Edwards, Coppicer

If anyone epitomises the face of Old England, it must be Lew Edwards. His weather-beaten countenance and knowing eyes are just the features that tales are made of. They reflect the strong character of someone who has spent his entire life in one small area, learning both to harness and harvest nature in due season, working with the elements but never trying to beat them. Still working at 80 years old, he is literally the old man of the woods, affectionately known to local children as 'Uncle Lew'. He is that countryman who used to work up every leafy lane. Now, however, his way of life seems remarkable when it is compared with that of most of us who rush about in stern competition for ever-diminishing resources, and who never quite learn to live in harmony with nature, as Lew has done so successfully.

Lew was born on 7 August 1912, in an estate cottage at Boundless Brickyard, about halfway between Godalming and Haslemere, in the Surrey hills. As a labourer for Lord Pirrie, Lew's father was helping at that time to build the fine wall which still stands around Witley Park. Clay was brought by horse and cart from lakes at nearby Grayswood village. 'Lord Pirrie bought everythin' inside the wall and gradually acquired other bits of land to make 4,400 acres', Lew told me. 'Some say 'e did good, and some say bad, but 'e did make a lot of employment.'

Nowadays, Lew cannot recall what his grandfather did, but he clearly remembers the first day that he met his grandmother. 'I was ten years old. We walked to Witley Station and caught the train to Godalming. From there we walked to Farncombe and on to Blackheath. When we got there she gave the old father a glass of home-made orange wine and me just a little thimbleful. By golly, it was good after all that walkin'. You never saw no bought wines in those days.'

Another rare commodity in the early twentieth century was the motor vehicle. Lew did not see a car until he was 4 years old, 'and that was in a ditch. It belonged to some doctor. The first Rolls Royce I ever saw was in a ditch, too, in the 1920s. It was a posh taxi effort and the driver 'ad taken a short-cut to see his parents. Trouble is, it was all soft verges in those days and they soon anchored you up.

'A lengthman looked after each stretch of road, and there was no lights except in towns. Most of the roads when I was a boy was no more than slugged-in stone, which was stone and fine gravel watered and watered until it settled down in a pulp. Up 'ere there was just a track. We didn't 'ave no tarred roads till the late Twenties.

'Everyone 'ad a pushbike in my young days: lots of 'em was the old 28in wheels – sort of puts you up in the air like. But it weren't too bumpy; the roads was reasonably looked after: the cars went quite slow and didn't tear up the stones. But you didn't know what rough was then because you 'ad never 'ad it smooth.

'We 'ad to walk 3 mile each way to Thursley school – up to the toll-gate on the A3, where we'd shout out "What's the time mister!", and then we knew whether to run to school or not. Any vehicle had to pay the toll.

'In those days it was crowded with little birds of all sorts. Once we 'ad an ol' butcher bird (red-backed shrike) in our 'edge at Boundless; she 'ad young birds an' insects stuck on the ol' thorn spikes. That was the only one I ever saw.

''Course, in those days there was so much more wildlife 'cos the vermin was all controlled. There was 28 keepers on the estate and it was nothin' for the Guns to get five or six hundred pheasants first day through on each beat. All the jays and magpies was killed – you hardly ever saw one, not like now, so there was plenty of small birds.

'There was also 'eaps of rabbits – it was our basic meal twice a week at least, and we often got a stoated one. Would 'ave been a pretty poor ol' livin' without that. No one ever 'ad much bought meat. Even if you kep' chickens you only ever 'ad one if you 'ad a spare ol' cockerel at Christmas.'

At the age of 12, Lew worked on summer evenings after school, at nearby Highfield Farm – 'choppin' up wood and generally 'elpin' out. They paid me 5s a week, but I think the main attraction was the nice tea they used to give me.

'When I was 14 I left school and went on for 'em regular, at 12s a week in the first year and 15s after that. They 'ad a dairy herd an' a few ol' Kent sheep for the winter. There was wheat, oats, barley, turnips for the sheep in winter, mangels for the cows, and a strip of trefoil was grown for cattle-feed – we used to get three cuts off that.

'My hours was eight to five Monday to Friday and eight to twelve Saturdays. Never 'ad no holidays either. I never stuck it all that long – ran away from farmin' at 16¾. I couldn't see no advancement to it. I heard of a job copse cuttin' – pea and bean sticks and tyin' up faggots, so I 'ad a go at that. This was workin' for Staffey Snelling at Heathflex Copse, which was part of Witley Park and now comes under the Forestry Commission.

'Then we got a job makin' a grass tennis court at Pook's Farm, Grayshott, and another at Headley. This was 1929, and I remember it well because that year we 'ad a severe gale which blew down 'undreds of elm trees all round 'ere: there was 27 down from Bowlhead Green up to the A3 alone. We 'ad an 8ft cross-cut saw and the trees was 7ft across. You couldn't give elm trees away then, there was so many about.

'Snelling paid me about 17 or 18s a week an' I worked about the same hours as on the farm. But it was a change. You can't say it was better – it was all 'ard work. It was gettin' that change in that counts – you felt you was gettin' somewhere.'

After that, it was back to where Lew was born, into Boundless Brickyard, where he worked at the sawmill. 'They 'ad this portable steam-engine which burnt all wood, an' I 'ad to stoke it up. The ol' thing leaked so much it didn't keep much steam up. Man called Jones owned it and I 'ad just two months there. He only went round tidying up all the dead wood – clearin' up the rubbish all the time.'

Next Lew went to work at Hydon's Ball, 'drivin' another steam-engine for a genuine sawmill supplyin' fencin' and buildin'. It took me three-quarters of an hour to get over there on me pushbike. I 'ad twelve months there, then the ol' gov'ner bought a big estate at Ifold, near Plaistow in Sussex, an' we went an' cut up all the ol' timber there. I still went by bike, but it took me between one and one-and-a-quarter hours. It weren't too bad goin' as the majority was downhill. I 'ad nine months there.

'We used to rely on stream water for the boiler, but one March it froze and froze and dried everythin' up into dust and it thawed out into dust, so we 'ad problems. That was about 1932 an' I've never seen anythin' like it since.

'Then the gov'ner got a contract to build a council-house estate and I was transferred to buildin' – knockin' up mortar for about ten bricklayers. But it was good pay I got there – 7d an hour. We was there a twelve month or more – see the job finished.

'Then it was over to Ardmore Estate, Guildford, to build private 'ouses. I was on general 'work – mostly hod carryin'. Then we went to Farncombe, and after that to Godalming, where we built 'ouses for £450 each in the mid-1930s. I suppose I stuck with the buildin' then because it was more entertaining. You was there with people and the time went quicker. On the farm you got stuck on a job on your own all day long.

'Then there was a job – all 'eard of by word-of-mouth in them days – where I thought I'd do better, for Milton's, convertin' a big ol' house into a school – the Naval. It took 18 months, then I went with Milton's to Greenhill's Farm, Fernhurst, where we pulled down the ol' house bar the chimney-stack and built a new place around it. It took six months and this was the first time I'd stayed away from home. I lived in a lodge with Laurie Coombs, retired keeper on the Blackdown Estate. Very nice, too, as it was next door to the pub and they treated me as though I were their son. I'd just asked for lodgin's in the pub – people was more interested to take you in then – everythin' was more genuine in them days.

'Mum died when I was 12, my two brothers went in the Army, I went away in lodgin's. One sister came back and tried to keep home for dad and me but couldn't manage and went away, and I've never seen her since. My other sister went in a home. In 1942

I thought I'd found my sister and answered a murder charge because the person 'ad a cut down the little finger and I'd given her one years ago. I said somethin' she didn't like, she went to box me ears and I put my knife and fork up to defend myself. But it wasn't her. After that the police did find her, but she didn't want to be known where she was.

'So it was just me and dad livin' together from about 1926 to 1943, till I got married and we came up 'ere to live with me in-laws. My wife died in 1969 and there's only my younger sister left as well as my daughter and son. See that ol' horse-chestnut there? My son brought it in as a conker from Redhill.

'When we moved out of the brickyard house at Boundless, Lord Pirrie knocked it down straightaway. He also owned Roundles Cottage, which we moved into; that was down in the bottom 'ere – was Cree Hole Farm – and we paid three bob a week rent.

'When I was a boy, there was no electricity, no toilets and no wash facilities. For washin' you 'ad to get water in a bucket from a well about 20yd outside the garden. Lightin' was all paraffin lamps an' candles, an' you 'ad to go easy with 'em: you 'ad to save anythin' in them days. Nothin' was plentiful. The only good thing was you could always get a bit of food of some sort. The grocer came round once a week, on a Friday from Milford Supply Store, and he'd take your order for next time. Summers the baker came out three times a week, on his horse and cart from Grayswood. My favourite was the ol' cottage loaf – no doubt about it. And on Good Friday they'd be up that much earlier so's the buns was still warm. The postman came on a bike from Godalming – all up through Brook. It was Tom Keen, who was born at Punchbowl Farm – was Pitt Farm. 'Course, there was quite a few letters then as there was more writin'. It only cost a penny a letter in those days.

'Heatin' was all wood, but you can't say it was free – it was all sweat money! You couldn't run about in the copses in those days and get a bit of wood just as you liked, especially as the keepers was so concerned for their pheasants. But on an estate they'd always cut a copse for firewood every winter. Whether the workers got it any cheaper I don't know. We needed quite a bit to heat the ol' copper.

'In my young days the place was lousy with gypsies – they used to camp on the common ground by Boundless Brickyard. They was forever comin' round and wantin' to buy a few eggs, but they kept their nose clean when they was settled.

'I remember once when I was playin' with one gyppo lad an"e pushed me over onto a broken jam-jar and the wound wouldn't heal. So father shaved off some Sunlight soap, mixed it with sugar and

bound it on the cut for three days. When 'e took it off it looked an awful mess, but we 'ad a big ol' black dog and 'e came up and started lickin' it clean till it was red raw again. Then dad made a ring bandage so it never touched the wound and from then on it started healin'.

'When I was 7 some gyppos came round for eggs when I 'ad 'oopin' cough bad. An ol' gyp told mum to get an ol' bread bun, wrap it up an' bury it for four days till it was mouldy and then give it to me to eat. I did just that and it worked – that's your penicillin. German measles – that was serious then – chicken pox – I've had the lot. But you was brought up bloody tough and came through it all right.

'When my son was seven 'e 'ad chicken pox an' it got inside is mouth. So I went to the pub an' took 'im back some cider an' next mornin' you could 'ardly see a spot in 'is mouth – it's the acid.'

After the job for Milton's at Fernhurst, Lew continued with the same builder as a general labourer. 'After a while, I asked Dick Milton if there was any chance of gettin' on with a trowel – bricklayin', an' I did. That was about 1934, and I continued with different builders till 1939, one of the big jobs I worked on being the Queen Elizabeth Barracks at Bordon.'

In 1939, Lew was out of work for three months, having decided to wait for a copse job with Hoptroff – 'the same firm I worked for at Hydon's Ball. The war began before I started, but I never signed on the dole because if you did it was straight in the Army, and I've never had a medical in me life.

So I started on the timber when I was 27, in charge of a gang, an' the ol' boy put in for my exemption, timber cuttin' bein' a reserved occupation. The wood was mostly put into railway sleepers and truck bottoms. All the material was ordered by the Ministry of Supply and most of our cuttin' was on the Witley Park estate. I had nearly five years there; there was masses of trees, some really fine timber, mostly oak. One man paid over a quarter of a million pounds for a load.

'There was three or four of us in a gang and it was all piece-work – so much a cube and we shared it all out. We worked about 8-5, Monday to Saturday, with axe and cross-cut saws, and I suppose I earned about £4 a week depending on the weather. Even in those days there still wasn't much meat to go round; the only blessing was if you kept a pig.'

At this time, Lew acquired some of his many scars and discovered just how dangerous timber-felling can be. Pointing to a scar on his wrist, he remembers: 'I 'ad the axe in there when I first started copse cuttin', an' I 'ad to walk all the way into Haslemere for stitches. Another time I was standin' on the top of a big ol' spruce tree we'd felled, strippin' the branches which slant back. I was chip-choppin' about and the axe touched

a bough up above an' came down across my foot, cuttin' the top off one of me toes. Anyhow, I 'ad an 'oliday then. They took me home an' the district nurse came out. In the evening I went by taxi to the doctor's and 'e asked who done me up. I said the district nurse an' 'e said right, that's good enough for me, so I could 'ave saved the price of the taxi!

BEYOND LIVING MEMORY

ROSES and elder-flowers find employment for the still; although our country ladies do not indulge themselves in the amusements of the still-room with the gusto of their grandmothers; their cordials of 'sovrain virtue' are almost forgotten; the present generation has almost lost its faith in five-leaved-grass water; and as for l'Esprit des Millefleurs, it is better from Delcroix 2 Paris. Peppermint is ready too for the still; — the camomile harvest, in Kent and Derbyshire, employs many children. Heath-berries of various kinds, as bilberries, cranberries, etc and mushrooms are gathered by the poor and carried for sale into the towns.

WILLIAM HOWITT
Book of the Seasons, 1830

'After the war I went back on the buildin', on a council pre-fab estate, at the top of Woolmer Hill, in Haslemere. We 'ad some bad weather then, about a dozen of us, but we was on piece-work and earned good money.

'Then I sort of chucked the buildin' in. I was gonna run a smallholding and rented a couple of fields the other side of Boundless. But then the Forestry Commission came in an' bought all the fields around, including mine behind my back. In fact, mine was the first they tore up. But they met with me to try and sort it out. At that time I could see the future in chestnut, so I said I'd let things be if I can have the chestnut as it comes up. So we went down the Dog and Pheasant, had a glass of beer and shook hands on it; an' it's been the same ever since. All my coppice has come from the Forestry Commission, but I did go outside once when I did walkin' stick stuff and needed three-year-old, which was 'arder to get. I supplied the Chalford Stick Company in Gloucestershire.

'I don't own or rent the copse, but pay a price for it when it's fit for cuttin', agreements bein' made with the local forester. There are people who'd come in an' cut your throat for it if they had the chance. As long as you pay a fair price you're all right. I suppose over the years I've paid between £30 and £300 an acre.

'All mine's used for post and pale fencing. Posts go to anyone, but all the pales go to Homewoods, chestnut fencin' manufacturers of Haslemere. I've always dealt with them; they started when I did and you could say we helped each other.

'A copse is cut any time from 12 years on. The piece I'm workin' on now is 19 year old and I've bought it three times over, spanning some 40 years. Nothin' much has changed in that time, except that the Forestry Commission's put respectable roads in. But all that land over there was just a field once. Most of the land round 'ere was first planted for the 'oop business and pheasant cover. I saw this bit cut for 'oops for barrels when I was 10 year old. My father-in-law planted a lot – 'e 'ad a long line with goose feathers on it to say where the trees was wanted. He worked for Lord Derby, who 'ad the estate before Lord Pirrie.'

Nowadays, Lew works from about eight until four, 'when I feels fit and the weather's right. I never try to beat the weather'. But he has some assistance, with one man helping with cutting and another part-timer who helps with wiring-up the fencing. In fact, the workplace in the woods is like a little factory, with bark-stripping machine and wood-splitting apparatus set up under a large blue plastic sheet, and piles of posts and finished fencing stacked neatly all around.

The copse is cut from November to March, when the sap is not rising. 'And the thicker it is the straighter and cleaner the stams [stems] are. Nowadays we take the lot down an' burn all the rubbish but in the old days the tops went for faggots. Most of the makin' up's done in the summer when there's no cuttin' and it's seasoned a bit, but we also make up straightaway, peelin', splittin', pointin' and wirin'.'

I asked Lew what he thinks about all day long and how he manages to cope with such hard physical work at his age. He replied: 'I likes work an' that's it an' all about it. To me it seems an achievement to do something worthwhile an' produce something. It's a challenge. I believe in livin' with nature and controllin' it, not like some of these idiots. Do you know, we've even had Jehovah's Witnesses up here; I pretty soon told 'em what my religion is – God is nature.'

But Lew has never been a recluse. Far from it; he still zips about the lanes in his Jetta car and is proud of the fact that he has 'a 62 year drivin' licence without a blemish on it.' 'ad me first motorbike when I was 17 years old, a Royal Enfield two-speed. And my first car was in 1940, a secondhand, two-seater Austin 7. When old [Sir] John Lee [then owner of Witley Park] saw my father 'e said, "Your son must be makin' some money, what with his car". But my dad soon put 'im right – 'e said, "It's only like bein' kicked by a donkey – pure ignorance".

'Father used to get over to the Red Lion at Thursley, and there weren't many nights he'd miss when we was at Boundless. He used to play cricket for Thursley and was the last man to bowl underarm for the team. I used to play cricket for Brook from when I was 16 till the war. And I played football for Brook and Grayswood United about the same time, nearly every Saturday and Sunday. I was in the second 11, but I haven't taken hold of a cricket-bat since the war.

'I only went for the social side really – a good ol' sing-song in the pub after. It was good in the pub then; if they were local people, you knew 'em. I remember goin' down the Dog and Pheasant on my 18th birthday and got chucked out the same night. And it weren't my fault either. They were good ol' days. If you 'ad half-a-crown in yer pocket you could face the evenin' comfortable. But many a time I went with a shilling. You'd buy the first brown for 4½d (we'd buy a pint and split it if we could, as it was cheaper at 7d), get on the ol' dartboard and if you won a couple of games you was all right as your beer was paid for. But if you lost, you 'ad to sit in the corner quiet like.'

SUPERSTITIONS AND CURES

THE PEOPLE of Tring, in Hertfordshire, would do well to remember, that no longer ago than the year 1751, and within twenty miles of the capital, they seized on two superannuated wretches, crazed with age, and overwhelmed with infirmities, on a suspicion of witchcraft; and by trying experiments, drowned them in a horse-pond. In a farm-yard near the middle of this village stands, at this day, a row of pollard-ashes, which by the seams and long cicatrices down their sides, manifestly show that, in former times, they have been cleft asunder. These trees, when young and flexible, were severed and held open by wedges, while ruptured children, stripped naked, were pushed through the apertures, under a persuasion that, by such a process, the poor babes would be cured of their infirmity. As soon as the operation was over, the tree, in the suffering part, was plastered with loam, and carefully swathed up. If the parts coalesced and soldered together, as usually fell out, where the feat was performed with any adroitness at all, the party was cured; but, where the cleft continued to gape, the operation, it was supposed, would prove ineffectual.

We have several persons now living in the village, who, in their childhood, were supposed to be healed by this superstitious ceremony, derived down perhaps from our Saxon ancestors, who practised it before their conversion to Christianity.

GILBERT WHITE
Natural History and Antiquities of Selborne, 1789

Having lived and worked in the same small area all his life, Lew has met some great characters, and even now, many years after they have gone, their voices still ring in this old countryman's ears. 'This bit we're on now was cut by George Madgwick and Squeaker West when I was 10. He was known as Squeaker because 'e 'ad a squeaky ol' voice an' you could 'ear 'im all over the woods, but he lived till gone 90. His son was the same age as me an' we used to go up there playin' about an' gettin' into mischief.'

And as well as the characters, the woods are full of incidents in Lew's life. 'In the war a string of bombs unloaded right down through 'ere. An ol' keeper found one 500-pounder just up there, while 'e was out settin' rabbit wires. They came an' took that away. But another one – I heard the thud – which was unexploded was never found. Neither has the one which fell in runnin' sand. For all I know they're out there now, an' there's people come up 'ere walkin' their dogs and enjoyin' the scenery.'

Almost every bush holds memories of wildlife, too, though in many places there are only ghosts where birds and animals once thronged. 'I 'aven't seen a nightjar for years, but when we was kids it was nothin' to 'ave five or six dodgin' you when you was cyclin' down Park Lane of an evenin'. An' I 'aven't 'eard a nightingale for God knows how long. These nature reserve people 'ave got it all wrong with their copse cuttin' and so on for wildlife. That's not the real problem. See, nowhere's keepered properly today. If a nightingale wants to be there, he'll be there, and a bloody ol' bramble patch is as good as anythin'.

'I got up to the first buzzard nest round here, you know. It was in a larch tree. In 1936 John Lee had 'em brought down from Scotland to control the rabbits on Witley Park, and they was all caged in to get 'em acclimatised. But when the war came there was no labour to do anythin' an' they was all turned loose, and they done well what with no keeperin' much durin' the war. There's still a few about. They're pretty quiet things down low – only time you 'ears 'em squakin' is up in the sky.

'Another thing you 'ardly ever see now is redstarts – you always used to see one round a farm buildin'. But there' still lots of adders around, and this year I've never seen slugs like it on these poles – they eat the algae. I remember one of the ol' charcoal-burners got bit up 'ere by an adder. They used to contract for whole woods up to the Fifties. But I only ever saw 'em with kilns. Even when I was a boy I never saw 'em earthin' up in the old way, though the marks was still in the woods where they'd been.

'Those ol' charcoal-burners was a rough lot – always gettin' a girl knocked up, an' there was one incident I always thought could 'ave led to a murder charge. One day there was three charcoal-burners workin' up 'ere reported another man missin' an' where he'd been workin' was blood on the ground. Well, when I saw the local policeman he said, "I hear there's a man missin' up your way". Later on, I thought, "I wonder if he's fallen down that well away over the back?", so I went to look. But I couldn't see anythin' because someone had jammed it tight with some thick ol' stams. After that the police found the missin' man some miles away walkin' along the road and claimin' he'd lost his memory. Well, I always wondered if he'd had a girl up demandin' money if he'd got her knocked up, done 'er in, dropped 'er down the shaft an' blocked it up. Far's I know, nobody ever did look.'

Nowadays, Lew's woods never ring to the crack of charcoal-burners, and only the occasional bark of a dog being exercised breaks the silence on Sundays. There was a time when just the gentle thud of Lew's light axe echoed about the coppice and birdsong filled the air. But now, on workdays the wild songsters are far fewer, and in any case you would often be hard-pressed to hear them because since the 1950s the chainsaw has dominated woodland work. And sometimes the sylvan silence is broken when Lew sparks up his 1951 Fordson Major tractor – 'one of the first'.

In all Lew's activities it is noticeable that he moves with a measured ease which enables him to work a full day into old age. Both mentally and physically, he works with nature and never against it. Even now he leaves younger, rush-and-tear men standing.

But for all the years and seasons he has seen and enjoyed, Lew's mark on the landscape will soon disappear as the woods close in after his inevitable passing and the disappearance of his way of life. The familiar figure from the woods of High Button will be but a memory and the cottage where he has lived alone for over 20 years will probably be modernised so that some nouveau countryman can move in without ever understanding the way rural life really was – tough and promising little in the way of material rewards, yet tremendously fulfilling in simple ways. And where geese and chickens now honk and cluck about the little garden, no doubt space will be made for the latest shiny company car.

Modern coppicing is an important means of retaining links with ancient wild woodlands. In addition to traditional hazel, birch, ash, willow, oak, field maple and hawthorn are all still actively coppiced in many parts of the country. And as well as providing a renewable, fast-growing source of wood in a sustainable environment, whilst extending the life of trees, a coppice is also a habitat in which wildlife can thrive. The sight of spring flowers covering the floor of a coppice is one of the most superb natural events, and coppices are home to some of Britain's rarer species, including dormice, nightingales and early purple orchids. As Oliver Rackham, acknowledged authority on woodlands says, 'woodmanship is an ecological factor in its own right'.

Today there are some 400 qualified craftsmen working as coppicers and The National Coppice Apprenticeship Scheme (www.greenwoodcentre.org. uk) encourages the continuation of the practice of coppicing. Its 'Week in the Woods' courses, held in a variety of locations, provide the opportunity to learn what coppicing involves, including 'tester' workshops. It also offers a three-year apprenticeship programme; at centres such as the Coppicewood College in Pembrokeshire (www.coppicewoodcollege.co.uk) it is possible to participate in shorter, six-month courses.

Yet one memorial to Lew is likely to last into the forseeable future. Down in Hampshire, at a pub called the Black Fox, on the A3 near Milland, is a stuffed black fox with a plaque bearing testimony to the man who trapped it – Lew Edwards. 'I caught it in 1965, on the same day Churchill died, and I hadn't seen it around the place before. I caught three foxes that morning and when my wife saw the black one she came out and said: "You bugger, you've caught someone's dog".

'Anyway, I 'ad it about the place here for a couple of days and then decided to 'ave it stuffed as a Churchill memorial. So I skinned it, put it in a box, took it to Hindhead Post Office and sent it to Mr Hare – that really was 'is name – at Golders Green. With the cabinet an' all, it cost £36, which was a lot in 1965. I drove up with a friend to collect it as 'e knew his way about up there.

'But when we got it, it was in the way a bit, and I used to pass the Black Fox when goin' down to visit my daughter in Hampshire. So I let the pub 'ave it on condition they gave me a letter statin' it was only on loan, which they did.'

Since then, Lew has not seen another black fox, 'but there's a white badger down here now, and in my time I've seen a white squirrel, white swallow and white blackbird'. And I believe every word Lew says because, by good luck, some months before we spoke, I too had seen that white badger while I was driving along the quiet lanes by Lew's house, on my way home late one night.

The black fox might be a rarity, but in these modern times it is less so than the man who caught it. Visitors to the Black Fox should realise that the name on the plaque is more remarkable than the creature displayed above it.

Lew Edwards died in October 2008, aged 96.

KING BEE

John Furzey, Professional Beekeeper

Having spent his entire working life as a professional beekeeper, you might say that Albert John Furzey has led a honeyed existence, but this would be far from the truth: John's life has been one endless round of long, unsocial hours, and hard physical work for only low wages. Yet his rewards have been great in terms of spiritual fulfilment, and as a result of his never-wavering passion for insects he has become one of the country's well-known authorities. Always ready to share his knowledge, he is constantly in demand as a speaker at bee society meetings.

Remarkably fit and glowing for his 58 years, John was born on 7 March, 1934 near the village of Combpyne, near Axminster, and he still retains a delightful Devon burr. 'Furzeys were as common as muck down there', he told me when we spoke at Clapper Hill, Ramsdell, near Basingstoke, his Hampshire country home since 1967.

John did not inherit his interest in bees from his family: his father was a gardener and his grandfather a carter and gardener. 'But I was always playing with insects and anything wild; there was so much more about then – lizards, newts, insects, birds and so on. And I collected all sorts, from eggs to beetles, stamps being my only thing away from the natural.

'One of my very earliest memories is going with an old lady – "Aunt", who lived next door – and finding a skylark's nest, and later we went blackberrying. She encouraged me a lot, but I was even luckier in being taught beekeeping at school – Axminster Secondary Modern, where, in the last year or so, we were split into three groups – rural, technical and commercial. I was in rural and we had beekeeping as a subject last period every Friday. The headmaster and science master took us. And I was close enough to belong to two local beekeeping associations. I always wanted to be a beekeeper. I suppose I didn't want to be a gardener, and if I couldn't be a beekeeper I wanted to be a warden or something to do with wildlife.

'In my last year or two at school I collected wasps' nests – dug 'em out without wearing a hat and veil. I'd put one in a biscuit-tin to study them and by the next morning they'd put a layer of "paper" right across. I'd leave it slightly open with a sheet of glass on top and throw another on top without any thought of them fighting.'

John did not start school until he was 6 – 'We lived right out in the wilds and there was no buses; it was only when we moved down into Uplyme village that I could go. Nobody had cars in them days.'

During the war years there were many evacuees in John's area. 'But we had a few bombs too, and I always remember when I was at the juniors, the secondary school got hit and all the kids had the day off. We was always goin' round in Jeeps with the Yanks. Sometimes Yanks would be out walking around the countryside and we would invite them in for a cup of tea on a Sunday afternoon.

'There was prisoners-of-war down there, too. They were Italians and we was always told to keep away from 'em, but they was a pretty friendly lot. There wasn't much security with 'em – a lorry used to come round and chuck 'em out at various points to do hedgin' and ditchin' etc on farms, and call back to pick 'em up at night. I suppose they knew they had nowhere to run to down there, or they didn't want to escape, but they was more careful with the Germans.'

When the time came for John to leave school, in April 1949, he told headmaster Tolchard that he wanted to work on a bee farm, and as a bee enthusiast himself, the head gave John great support. 'First he wrote to Lt-Col Goring at Whimple, the old Whiteways cider place, but they had no position, and a good job I didn't go there too, as they closed down two years later. Then he wrote to Brother Adam, the famous beekeeper at Buckfast Abbey, but he said no because only monks did the work there, and I certainly didn't want to be a monk. But Brother Adam suggested Alec Gale, so we wrote to him and as a result I went to Marlborough for three months' trial.'

When John first went to Gale's he was a little disillusioned, having to spend the entire first week in a shed cutting up old sacks for smoker fuel. 'Someone said, "All you do is chop 'em up the size of a pocket handkerchief", but I can tell you that by the end of the week the handkerchief was pretty big in my eyes! During that first seven days I didn't even see a hive.

'Gale's had at least a dozen men and was considered the biggest bee farm with fifteen or sixteen hundred hives, but it stayed about that size.

'I started on 44s for a 47-hour week in 1949, and out of that I had to pay 35s lodging and 2s 10d insurance. That left me with the princely sum of 6s 2d spending. I lodged with Gale's company secretary.

'At first I was smoker boy, which meant general dogsbody, to any gang, and at Gale's this lasted three years, during which time I was bossed by anybody and everybody. Generally, we ended up working 60 to 70 hours a week, but in the first year I had about 1s 2d an hour overtime, later going up to 1s 10d.'

In 1952 John had to do his National Service, which meant two years in the Royal Army Service Corps, 19 months of that time being spent at Munster, in Germany. 'The bulk of the chaps put on this great show of bein' tough, but most of 'em was townies and dead scared of creepy-crawlies. Once we was camped in a wood and I found a bumble-bees' nest which I dug out and threw in an old tin. As soon as I touched it, not one of those "brave" chaps was to be seen.

'I took the bees back to the barracks and they stayed there quite happily, till one day the sergeant went by, spotted the tin and gave it a kick. Out came the bees and away he went in a mighty hurry. But by then all the other lads was used to 'em so they had a good chuckle over it with me.

'One autumn night in Germany I was on guard duty and it seemed that everything was out to spook me. First there was this strange noise along the road, but it turned out to be only the leaves rustling along. Then I spotted a mysterious glow in the forest, but when I approached it turned out to be some of that luminous fungus which grows on trees. The only other time I saw that was on a stump near here, when I was out walking the dog one night.'

In 1954, after completing his National Service, John returned to Gale's – 'they were obliged to give me my job back'. There he thrived with the company. 'All through the war and in the 1950s and 1960s was generally good for bees and Gale's did well.'

However, in 1967, two years before Alec Gale died, John left to work at Clapper Hill Bee Farm for David Rowse, where he looked after some 500 hives. 'Mr Rowse sold to Honey Farmers in 1981 and I became manager for them until they sold back to David Rowse in 1986. Then in 1989 he sold to Alan Willens and when he packed up in April 1991 I was made redundant, Alan Willens moving his operation to Andover.' John still lives in the bungalow at the bee farm and is attempting to set up his own business of queen rearing as well as producing a small amount of honey and doing contract gardening. During the 43 years he has extracted the best from bees, he has seen many changes.

In the early 20th century, disease – popularly known as the Isle of Wight epidemic – caused the loss of some 90 per cent of bee colonies within the British Isles and by the end of World War I the old native

English bee was gone, as was traditional keeping of bees in skeps (straw or wicker hives). And while Brother Adam played a leading role in the adaptation of imported varieties, Alec Gale, for whom John worked for 18 years, spearheaded the business side to maximise honey production.

FIRESIDE OCCUPATIONS

IN LARGE farmhouses, many useful avocations may enliven the evening fireside. In some districts, the men mend their own clothes and shoes; in others, various repairs of smaller implements, as flails, sieves, etc. are done; and it is now become a laudable custom in many superior farms, to encourage reading, and other means of mental improvement, which the continual engagements of a rural labourer preclude during the summer. The promotion of this spirit is highly to be desired; no part of our working population having been so lamentably deficient in common knowledge as that of farmers' servants. Through the summer they have toiled from morning till night, and from day to day incessantly; and their only intervals of rest, Sundays and winter nights, have been lost in drowsiness. The cottager may usefully, by his winter fire, construct bee-hives, nets, mole-traps, bird-cages, etc.

WILLIAM HOWITT
Book of the Seasons, 1830

'When I was at Gale's, the poorest crop was 18 tons and the best 90. Most was put in jars but some sold – in bulk.' But then there was still plenty of clover and what John misleadingly calls 'rubbish' – the 'general wild flowers' for the bees to feed on. 'It was not till the mid-1960s that there was much rape and since then the honey quality has deteriorated. Just a year ago I had some off an uncle and I said to him this is just how it used to taste.

'Mind you, heather honey still tastes as it used to – that's my favourite. And I think Exmoor honey is better than Scottish. Mind you, it's dearer than flower honey by about 40-50 per cent. I like to eat honey when I'm extracting and chew away on it all the time – much better than when it's jarred. Rape honey is just like sugar and water – not much taste to it. Cherry honey is very nice, but now they've cut most of the trees down.'

At Gale's, trees were an important part of the business, which also owned a farm and woodland. 'In winter we went up to the woods to dig Christmas trees. This meant they could keep on staff all the year, and I used to drive all over the country delivering these trees. But there was also a lot of maintenance work in winter.'

John's year really starts in March, when he takes the woodpecker nets and guards off the hives. The half-inch wire-mesh guards and loosely fitted nets over pairs of hives pushed together ('that saves one wall from attack') are essential to protect against green woodpeckers, which are always on the lookout for an easy insect meal in winter, when food is scarce. 'People have actually caught a pecker inside a hive where they've made a hole big enough. One year a friend in Sussex had some 90 out of 200 hives damaged by peckin'. Then again, there's mice gets inside in the winter; they'll eat all the combs and suchlike and ruin 'em.'

BEE BOY

WE HAD in this village more than twenty years ago an idiot-boy, whom I well remember, who, from a child, showed a great propensity to bees; they were his food, his amusement, his sole object. And as people of this cast have seldom more than one point in view, so this lad exerted all his few faculties on this one pursuit. In the winter he dozed away his time, within his father's house, by the fireside, in a kind of torpid state, seldom departing from the chimney-corner; but in the summer he was all alert, and in quest of his game in the fields, and on sunny banks. Honey-bees, humble-bees, and wasps, were his prey wherever he found them: he had no apprehension from their stings, but would seize them nudis manibus, and at once disarm them of their weapons, and suck their bodies for the sake of their honey-bags. Sometimes he would fill his bosom between his shirt and his skin with a number of these captives; and sometimes would confine them in bottles. He was very injurious to men that kept bees; for he would slide into their bee-gardens, and, sitting down before the stools, would rap his fingers on the hives, and so take the bees as they came out. He has been known to overturn hives for the sake of honey, of which he was passionately fond. As he ran about he used to make a humming noise with his lips, resembling the buzzing of bees. This lad was lean and sallow, and of a cadaverous complexion. When a tall youth he was removed from hence to a distant village, where he died, as I understand, before he arrived at manhood.

GILBERT WHITE
Natural History and Antiquities of Selborne, 1789

With the nets off, the stocks (the professional's name for hives) are pushed apart and John sees the bees for the first time since November. 'Usually, in winter we only lose a few stocks – mainly drone layers and queenless; we never get any starved.' Indeed, keeping the bees in top condition is John's priority throughout the year.

Since the mid-1970s, he has regularly used pollen supplement to get the bees off to a good start. 'This is the easiest way to stimulate them, and with the winter rape comin' on so early, we've got to do something to make 'em breed quick. Any queenless and drone-laying stocks soon become evident because they very seldom take the pollen supplement.'

The supplement is made by mixing 1 lb each of honey, syrup and brewer's yeast, which are heated to 120°F, removed from the heat and stirred with a little under 2 lb of defatted soya flour and a little irradiated, imported pollen. 'We've spent years gettin' this recipe right and it is important that it should not be too dry, but thick and substantial, so that each patty can be placed directly on the top bars of the hive and won't push down between the combs. I put on the first lot in the first week of March and a second cake two weeks later. The-bees take it very quickly and a large stock is given a 2 lb patty every time. Years ago, before winter rape, this wasn't so important as there was no main honey flow that early, though you'd sometimes get a bit in May. Now half the crop comes off rape; one year we had 7 tons off it, but only 4 in the summer.'

As John goes around the hives, he can immediately sense what state the bees are in: 'There'd be quite a roar to them if they was queenless, buzzin' around and runnin' all over the place. In the winter you've got to give 'em plenty of air, but in the spring condense 'em down and wrap 'em up warm to encourage 'em to breed. If there are any combs without any bees on I put these outside the dummy so that you get your bees on six or seven frames.'

Each queen has to have its wings clipped to help overcome swarming. 'Now I snip across both wingtips, but at Gale's we used to clip just half of one wing off. A swarm would be found in the grass or under the hive. Frequently, the bees desert the queen, then she would be dead nearby. This just gives us a few days' grace as they'd have to hatch a young queen before they'd swarm again. And if a swarm gets into a hole in a building you won't get 'em out – might as well kill 'em.'

Every one of John's stocks has a record card which is meticulously kept up-to-date so that its history is always to hand. 'Some people use books, but I've seen this book lark – you leave it back at the yard, so you scribble away on any old bit of paper and that very soon gets lost.'

March is also the time to clean and change the hive floors – John treats his thoroughly with a safe form of Cuprinol every third or fourth season. Equipment from dead stocks must be cleaned and the hive, floor, entrance block and inner cover all scorched with a blow-torch, especially in crevices. Combs are treated with acetic acid, but they are well aired before eventual use.

In spring the professional beekeeper is on the alert to take his strongest stocks down to Kent, to assist in the pollination of 'The Garden of England', and traditionally he has been paid for his trouble. In most years there is not a great honey flow from the apple and pear orchards, but what there is, plus the fruit-grower's payment, can make it very worthwhile. As John says, 'You could keep 'em home and have a good crop off the rape, but in a poor year, when the weather's against you, you could end up having to feed 'em a lot and make a loss.

'On the commercial side you've got to be really committed, it's no good being one of those "let alone" beekeepers. In summer you should go round every hive every nine days and you should have decent stocks by the end of April. With no bees you get no honey – simple as that, no mystery to it. You know straight away if a stock's wrong. All the time you're asking yourself, "Is there a decent brood nest, is the queen all right, is there sufficient food, any sign of disease, is there enough pollen?" Very often you only have to look at one comb to see you've got a decent queen. You've got to push 'em along all the time.

'One thing I do know is that the bee's character varies a hell of a lot. I even take a liking to some queens. You could say that I do everything by instinct, but then I have been with the bees all my life. There's no way you can teach a townie beekeeping – you must be genuinely interested in wild things, which bees are, of course.

'Anyway, they usually go down to Kent for six weeks or so, from about 20 April to the end of May. And the farmers will tell you precisely when they want them. So you need to be prepared to work at unearthly hours – even in the dark – to catch all the bees while they are in and load 'em up for their long journey.' Course, some people go on and on about the stress for the bees, but I don't think movin' em upsets 'em. Quite the opposite really, because when they come back from Kent they're usually really strong stocks.

'At Gale's we used to go down to Kent for up to six days and I have worked 99 out of 144 available hours, often up at 4am and a midnight finish. In recent years I've had up to a hundred stocks on the Land-Rover and trailer, but that slows you down a bit. Normally, I'd carry 64 stocks on the trailer and 6 in the back of the Rover. With a medium 2-ton load you could cruise very nicely on the motorway at 50mph. Luckily, I've never had any great mishaps. I've lost the odd hive off the back but soon gathered it up. You've got to make sure that the hives are bee-proof, but floatin' around the vehicle. Never bothered me, but some passengers can get rather excited.'

Despite his wealth of experience, John has no special immunity to bee-stings, but does have a sixth sense when it comes to potentially painful situations – most importantly, when you are loading the hives, 'There is no need to take any notice of the ones comin' back – they're the workers, poor little devils. It's the ones comin' out that's gonna sting you!

'When I was at Gale's the men often went home at night with their arms so swollen with stings their overalls was-tight. It was nothing for a man to get 200 or 300 stings in a day, but that was much less than one a minute, so not too bad. Now I wear gloves most of the time and usually only get stung 20 or 30 times a day. It's very important not to be so togged up you never get stung at all and do not have any immunity; best to build, up gradually at the start of the year.

'It still bloody hurts me. I always remember one little sod went right in my ear – in reverse! At Gale's, on a nice day some of the men would strip off to the waist, with only a veil and trilby on top, and old Alec hardly ever wore a veil. Funny thing is, our basic gear was blue overalls when all the books say you should wear white. But I didn't leave there for the stings – I went for a better job.'

Quite apart from the stings, the professional beekeeper 'hasn't got to be a weakling', says John. 'I suppose these stocks, without supers, weigh three-quarters' of a hundredweight apiece, and the number of times I have to lift 'em about I wouldn't like to guess.' The weight of honey alone is considerable. 'One year I averaged 50lb per colony on rape and some years you get the odd stock bringing in up to 200lb.

'We take the honey off at the end of May or beginning of June, when the rape is over. I like to think that we do a bit of good on the rape. A lot of people say that rape's just wind pollinated, but I've always thought that the bees make just that 5 per cent difference to the crop. Anyway, rape honey granulates pretty quickly, and when it's off we have a lot of combs to scrape back to the foundation.

'After the rape is over we come to what is known as the June gap, when there is very little income unless there are field beans close by, so you have to watch that bees don't starve at this time. Trouble is, beans are usually coming into flower before the apples are finished, and as most farmers like the bees around at this time you sometimes have to be a bit of a diplomat keepin' them all happy. But sometimes I get grumbled at.

'A small feed will keep the bees going, but it may also encourage swarming. In most years many stocks need feeding in June, and once I fed up to 10 July, when most stocks were starving, but ended up with a good crop in late July and early August.'

At Clapper Hill Bee Farm John has been used to feeding in very large quantities. 'Seventeen inches of water are put into the bottom of the 6ft diameter syrup-maker, inside which is a paddle which revolves just about 50 times a minute. The water is heated to 100°F and 50cwt of sugar added to make 660 gallons of syrup. This only

SECURING SWARMS

THERE IS something very picturesque in the manner of reclaiming the swarms of bees. Their departure is announced for a day or more before it takes place by an unusual bustle and humming in the hive. Some person, commonly a boy, is set to watch; and the moment their flight is proclaimed, a ringing is commenced upon a pan or fire-shovel, which, as country people say, charms them down. They alight, or rather the queen-bee alights, upon the end of a bough; and the rest of the bees clustering, or as it is termed knitting, about her, form a living brown, dependent cone. Beneath this some adroit operator spreads a cloth (upon a table if one can be had), and holding an empty hive inverted under the swarm, suddenly shakes them into it, and places it, with all the captive colony in it, upon the cloth. In this state they are conveyed to the place they are intended to occupy; and the following morning they are found to have taken kindly to their new dwelling. They will frequently fix themselves to the roofs of houses.

It is a superstition common both in France and in this country, to-announce to the bees the death of the master of the family; in some places, of any individual of the family; or it is believed the bees would die, or fly away. It is also reckoned unlucky to sell bees, in some places; and for this reason, when a person parts with a hive, he will not receive its value in money, but stipulates for a certain part of its produce.

WILLIAM HOWITT
Book of the Seasons, 1830

takes about one and a half hours and the syrup is pumped into outside tanks taking 3,000 gallons. We used to make this up during the last week of August and start feeding in the first week of September.

'Ten tons of sugar would last a year and we used the Rowse Miller-type feeder taking 3 gallons and covering the whole top of the hive. If you feed heavily in the autumn, then feeding is rarely required in the spring. Some people try to save on a bit of sugar and wonder why they don't get much honey. They give very little winter feed after robbing their bees and I believe that such people should be starved.

'The June gap is the time to use bees and brood to make nuclei, etc. Some people just can't be bothered and go out to buy what they want, but that's very expensive. To start again after a bad winter you want to divide. Run the stocks for honey right the way through till the end of July, then halve and give the queenless part a cell or young queen. It means you've got to rear some queens or get some cells from somewhere. If I wanted, say, a hundred hives, I'd buy about ten in spring, run them for early honey and make a lot of nucs, put 'em on winter rape, get big stocks in June, then split each stock into two-frame nucs and give a cell, probably bought in. There's no end of ways of making increase.'

Despite his great authority, John readily admits 'When three beekeepers are gathered together you will hear three ways of doing every job there is.' As a result, his opinions are keenly sought for the columns of magazines such as *Hampshire Bee Talk*. And his bookshelf bulges with the writings of other beekeepers, as far back as the Victorians. John knows them all almost as well as he knows the inside of a hive, but perhaps none more intimately than *Teach Yourself Bee-keeping* by Lt-Col A N Schofield, inscribed: 'Awarded to

John Furzey by Axminster Secondary Modern School, Christmas, 1948, H B Tolchard, headmaster'.

Since those early days there have been many changes of opinion in the beekeeping world, but very few significant changes in equipment. 'It is still of the utmost importance to keep the hive clean', says John, 'and to wage war on the enemies of bees such as the greater wax moth, whose grubs hide in all the cracks and can ruin a hive. And nowadays ministry inspectors make regular checks for disease – some 30 per cent of all hives in an area each year. But a clean bill of health doesn't mean you can forget it and relax; you've got to be on your toes all the time. As one MAFF foul-brood officer said to me, "It's like the MOT really – it's all right at the time". Disease is usually spread by the beekeeper or robbing. A colony might go wild, have disease and die out and a strong stock would rob its tree, bringing disease back home.'

With the main flowering in July and early August, the honey flow really gets going, 'and in some areas this can be big off all sorts of rubbish, including thistles, brambles and willow-herb; they even rely on it in some areas. But whatever crop you're at, don't keep the hives in a straight line as you then get a lot of drifting of bees from one hive to another and end up with really strong stocks on the ends and weak ones in the middle.'

One traditional way to keep the honey flowing after the main flowering has ended is to take the bees to heather. Not only does this produce some of the most delicious and commercially valuable honey, but also it reduces the feed bill, which is an important consideration for the professional. Because of the long distance often involved, it is obviously important to take as many bees as possible and to select only the strongest stocks.

John has been taking bees down to Exmoor, Dartmoor and the New Forest (and once to Yorkshire) since August 1949. 'The youngest son of the farmer who owned the field where I first went on Exmoor was only 25 then, but now he's thinkin' of retiring. And they've still not repaired the gate to that yard' (the professional's name for the site where a group of hives is placed).

'We'd select the best stocks from each yard and these would be subject to three checks before the heather trip. First time the bees would be checked and the clearer boards (for getting the bees out of the honey supers) put on. Second time we'd take the honey off and put a feeder on. We always ensure that each lot has nine frames of brood and masses of bees. Third time round the feeder is taken off and a gauze screen screwed on top – with lots of bees crammed in it is essential that they have plenty of air on the journey, so we travel with the roofs off. We also have to sprinkle them with water to keep cool as the journey is made in the heat of early August. We'd travel all through the night and be in position by dawn, before the heat was up and the bees active.

'You don't want to stay near the bees after you've let 'em out as they don't take kindly to being cooped up and you'd soon get a few stings.

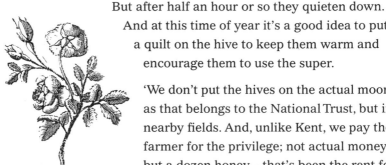

But after half an hour or so they quieten down. And at this time of year it's a good idea to put a quilt on the hive to keep them warm and encourage them to use the super.

'We don't put the hives on the actual moor as that belongs to the National Trust, but in nearby fields. And, unlike Kent, we pay the farmer for the privilege; not actual money but a dozen honey – that's been the rent for as long as I can remember. But it's certainly well worth it: over the years I've averaged 30lb a hive, and in 1981 we had over a ton off 32 in one field. Usually half a ton is good off that number. And between the time we take them down and when we bring them back about 20 September, we usually only make one visit, after a couple of weeks, to make sure everything's all right.

'Heather brings the last real chance in the year to make honey. You want a sheltered spot for the yard, but the bees will put up with quite a bit of wind when working heather. Trouble is, it's gettin' harder all the time to find suitable sites. Mind you, transport's much easier now – in the old lorry and with the roads not half so good, 30mph was the best we could hope for. One other little snag is that heather honey is usually harder to get out of the combs and must be pressed so the combs often have to be scraped. We usually scrape them back to the centre rib and then let the bees draw them out again.'

After all the effort with the heather and many nights working until 10 pm or later in August, moving stocks in from temporary sites to permanent yards, October brings welcome relief for John. 'This is my quiet time and at last I can take my "summer" holiday. But there have been times when I could take my rest earlier, such as in September 1976, when there was nothing to do. The record drought brought the worst season I can remember – we had only 9 ton 18cwt that year. There was a good crop early on, but everythin' dried up by July and many of the bees would have starved if we hadn't fed them during the late summer. We didn't bother to go to the heather that year.

'Our average crop from 500 stocks in 1968–76 was 16 ton 17cwt, but then things started to deteriorate, I think because of the switch from summer rape to winter rape, which is in flower from April so the bees aren't so strong. With summer rape there's a nice time to build up to give a massive stock.

'My best year was in 1971, with 22 ton 15cwt, and we never took any bees to Exmoor that year as we was so busy.'

Not surprisingly, the worst winter John can recall was record-breaking 1962-3, 'when Gale's had 400 stocks dead out of 1,600. It wasn't the severe frost that-killed 'em off, but they were under snow for weeks on end and there was no chance for breeding in March. Two or three of the yards wintered well, which was odd as they was in unusual places facing north. 1968-9 was bad, too, with 25 per cent losses. I think that was because in early August 1968 there was no brood in the stocks, so only old bees went into the winter.'

In November John has to tidy all the yards up, trimming back nearby undergrowth and generally making good. 'This takes a couple of weeks, but sadly, many keepers don't bother. And, of course, it's time to put the woodpecker guards and nets on again.' Some 15 years ago, John had massive holes pecked in ten to 12 hives in just one yard. 'And that was with nets on, so we had to give the place up. But the human is the worst predator – some even tip hives over. Wasps are no great problem if you have a strong stock – any raiders will soon be repelled.'

With any luck, John will have completed his winter preparations by the end of November, having battened down the hatches, collected all the record cards and delivered the rent honeys. 'If it's mild it's a bloomin' nuisance, as some of the bees will still be flyin'

about and as soon as you touch 'em they're straight out. I like it to be nice and frosty so that they're all bunched up inside and clustered and I don't have to bother with a veil.'

After that, John probably won't see the bees until March, unless he is out and about in the car and curiosity gets the better of him, which it often does. Most of the winter he spends indoors, repairing equipment.

As for the honey, 'That's always been sold to whoever pays the most for it' – in 6cwt barrels on the farm, but nowadays he also sells it by the jar at car-boot sales, 'and there's a good profit to be had in buying it in, packaging it up neatly and selling it on. It wasn't worth the farm bottling much if they could get a good bulk price from big packers.'

The bee-farm separator yielded great piles of wax, 'mostly sold for making foundation for new combs, but some went to makers of furniture polish and candles.

'Nowadays the Bee Farmers' Association says anyone with over 40 stocks is commercial, but I would say at least 100. There can't be more than 20-30 full-time beekeepers in this country. It's been gettin' harder and harder and I wouldn't advise anyone to go into it. In the old days Galc's would take 1,000 stocks down to

Kent and back and then put up to 40 stocks in one place for the summer and forget them until it was time to go to the heather. And on Exmoor we had 70 in one yard. But now the heather's got less and all the foraging has diminished generally. Everythin's got worse for us. Winter rape's helped a bit and you can sometimes put 20-30 stocks in one place, but only for brief periods. In 1949 we had an average of 118lb from the 1,000 stocks that was runnin'. Even so, I can see room for people who are prepared to work very hard and look after, say, one hundred stocks of bees-a husband-and-wife team perhaps, but with another job.' John himself is lucky in having his wife Maureen to cater for bee society visits.

John does not have much time for 'royal jelly' – the mysterious food given by young bees to the selected larva, enabling an otherwise ordinary larva destined to be a mere worker to head the colony. It's said to have special health-giving qualities, but John says: 'You'd need a bucketful to do any good. It's 'orrible stuff; most of it comes from China and I'm told some of it contains pesticides. Anyway, I wouldn't want the job of collectin' it; I don't think there's much real stuff in what you buy. But propolis-bee glue – is supposed to be good. It's the stuff that

sticks everything in the hive together and we used to get £2 an ounce for it. I know one chap who bought a good Volvo on it – not a new one, though – some ten years ago. And you have to scrape it off the equipment anyway.

BEEKEEPING TODAY

 With millions of honeybees being killed each year by disease, there is more interest than ever in beekeeping and the establishment of new, healthy colonies everywhere from back gardens and allotments to meadows and heathlands. As the British weather pattern – and farming practice – have changed over the years, so too has beekeeping. Today, beekeepers usually start opening their hives in March, with the first honey being taken out of the hive in late April or early May. The main honey crop is taken from the hive in July or early August. In areas where rape is grown its pollen produces literally tons of honey, a good reason to welcome rather than denigrate this crop which paints the spring countryside bright yellow. In many districts, particularly close to moorlands, beekeepers will have a later crop of heather or ivy honey, which is taken off in September. As well as honey, the hive will produce wax, which is ideal for crafting wonderfully fragrant homemade candles and polishes.

It is not difficult to get started as a beekeeper, but it is wise to receive advice from other, experienced beekeepers before you begin, and to be fully equipped with everything from hives to protective clothing – and of course a healthy swarm. The best source of information of all kinds is The British Beekeeper's Association (www.britishbee.org.uk) which, with The International Bee Research Association (www.ibra.org.uk), is particularly concerned with ensuring the future of our honeybees.

To survive in the business for so long, John has had to be a good judge of both human and insect character. But with the bees, 'I think a decent hybrid Italian is about the best one. I've tried most of 'em in my time. These quiet New Zealand ones which people seem to think do well I've found completely useless. Then there's American – you can practically pick 'em up, with no fuss, but they done nothing. I've had Israeli without success; the Swiss only give about 20 lb of honey before swarming, and the French are some of the most vile-tempered ones you can get.'

But no matter how 'angry' the bees, you could easily imagine John Furzey charming them down from the trees. He has the warmth of character to get on with anyone. And if the Bee Farmers' Association saw fit to invite him to lecture, then he must also be worth listening to.

John Furzey retired and sold his
bees in May 2008, at the age of 74.

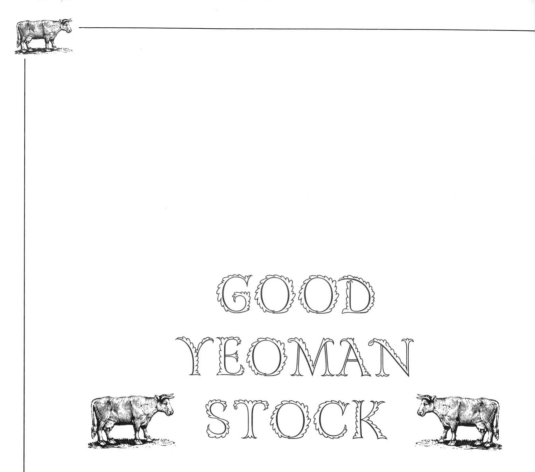

GOOD YEOMAN STOCK

Kenneth Liverton, Farmer

'I ALWAYS wanted to be a farmer; there's nothin' to take its place', 77 year-old Ken Liverton told me at his Woolbeding, Sussex, home which has origins in the 11th century. But then, that is not surprising when both his father and grandfather were also tenant farmers before him. And now his only son follows in the family tradition. 'Mind you, my two brothers weren't too interested, but they came back to it after the war.'

The family's roots are in Devon, 'but it was hopeless to get a farm early this century', so Ken was born – on 15 March, 1915 at Cams Hall, Fareham, Hampshire, where his father had to be content with running an estate. 'From Fareham we went to live at Staines, as dad took on a milk business when I was five, and when I was eight he got North End Farm, at Liphook, in Hampshire.'

'Everythin' was so quiet then – only the odd car or two chasin' around. No tractors – all horses. Most places it was quite safe to be on the road. Only trouble was when the occasional horse and trap bolted.

'Nothin' was ever wasted then. As soon as a horse dropped his fuel, out ran the old ladies with their shovels; some always watched the milk trap and as soon as the horse cocked his tail out they'd go.'

It was also a time when farming was more sympathetic towards wildlife and Ken always found time to give nature a helping hand. One incident stands out from the days when he first started to help his father on the farm. 'I was runnin' a light pair of harrows over some corn 2-3in high, to get rid of the weeds, when I saw a plover up ahead on its nest. So I carried on till the horses drew close, walked over, picked up the eggs, put them in my pocket, marked the spot with a stick, carried on down the field, came back and went over the nest with the harrows. Then I stopped again and dug out a depression with my hand, where the stick was, put in a few bits of stubble straw as lining and then the eggs. I then worked up and down a bit and the bird came back and sat on the nest. I was very pleased about that.

'You see, in those days you really saw wildlife. Once you got your first furrow made and the horses were set in you could relax and watch everythin' around you.'

APRIL TASKS

FEEDING cattle in the yard still continues, from deficiency of grass. Fields are cleared of stones, bash-harrowed, and shut up; all ditching, hedging, and draining, better done last month. Water meadows, which have been eaten, closed at the end of the month. Sowing still continues of spring corn, peas, tares, sainfoin, lucerne, and grasses; also the sowing and planting of woad, madder, flax, hemp, mustard, rape, poppy, rhubarb, and other medicinal plants; at the end of the month planting mangel-wurzel, carrots, and Swedish turnips. Early potatoes are planted. Hops are poled, and the ground between the rows dressed. Evergreens are planted, as holly, yew, and the fir tribes. Poultry broods are hatched, and demand much of the good housewife's care

Dairy Time

ABUNDANCE of grass plunges the housewife into the cares and processes of the dairy, skimming, churning, and cheese-making. The farmhouse is now an affluent place, abounding in the good things made from milk; rich cream, sweet butter, curds, curds and cream, syllabubs, custards, and so forth. Where there is a dairy, at this season, fetching up cows, milking, churning, scouring utensils – making, pressing, and turning cheese, etc. leave no lack of employment. Osiers are peeled; and it is pleasant to see groups seated in the open air at this employment. The garden demands weeding, training, and putting in flower-seeds. The children of the poor gather cowslips for wine. Poultry broods demand attention; corn is weeded, and rearing calves turned out.

WILLIAM HOWITT
Book of the Seasons, 1830

Of course, in those days farm boys were always expected to help out after school, 'and before we went in the morning we had to milk two cows each, by hand. Us boys were only allowed to deal with the quiet cows, but I did have a bit of trouble one morning. I was sitting on the stool, bucket between my legs, as usual, and it was very warm and sunny with a lot of flies about. I suppose one of 'em stung my cow so she picked up her foot and bumped my bucket. I grabbed the bucket and stool but immediately she picked up a foot again and put it straight down on my foot, breakin' the arch. And I daren't let go of the bucket. Anyway, you didn't go to the doctor in those days, so I just had to put up with it. I've had a troublesome callous under my foot ever since.'

The milk was cooled and put into 17 gallon churns for daily collection by a lorry with solid-rubber wheels, which took it to Petersfield. 'You don't get milk like it now – they kill everything in it with treatment. When I was a boy it was good for making cream, cheese and butter, and mother was always busy.

'She made wonderful clotted cream. Now the doctors say it's bad for you, but I bet I've eaten more Devonshire cream than anyone else. Mother took a pan of about 2 gallons of our fresh milk in the morning and let it stand till evening, when she'd put it on the old range on a low heat, gradually bringing it up over half an hour or so but never letting it boil. Then off it came and back in the larder. Next morning she'd go round the edge of the pan with a knife and take the crust off into a fair-sized basin. My father always said I'd get sick of it, but I never did. In those days the wife had to be able to cook and store anything as there were no fridges.'

Ken left school at the age of 14 to help his father on the farm, 'working all the hours of daylight and for no pay. I 'ad to catch rabbits for my pocket money. I made and set my own snares – got good at it, too, eventually having about 50 down. After a while we met this chap who was in with the Navy and said he'd take as many as I could get. They were all hamstrung then and all I had to do was tie them up in dozens, label them for House & Son, Gosport, and put them on the train at Liphook – imagine doing that today. Then I'd be sent a cheque, but I had no bank account, so father had to bank it and he said, "We'll have to go halves on this" – times was really bad on the farm then. I think we got about 6d a rabbit.

'I also used to do a lot of pigeon-shooting. They used to play havoc with our flat pole cabbage – damn great things which was fodder for the cows. We 'ad about 4,000 plants up from Devon each year and planted them about a foot apart. They did well coming from that red Devon soil into ours.

'One day when I was 17, mum and dad were out and I was in charge. There was a small field by our cowshed and in there was a lot of dandelions, which I spotted an ol' woman pickin'. Well, being in charge I thought I'd better do something about it. But I didn't like to just go out and say something. Anyway, in the cowshed we used to keep an old bull, so I went down and untied him and let him out the side door into the dandelion field. As he went out I crept along and looked out the cowshed window. Well, 'e came round the corner and went "Brrr". She took one look and was off, and there was a barbed wire fence there which she got all hooked up in.

'When she was gone, I just put a bit of cake in the yard, I called out, "Come on, Bill", in came the bull good as gold and I tied him up again. I'd never do that now.

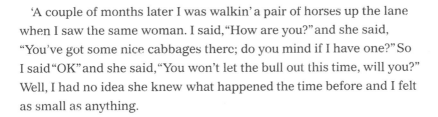

'A couple of months later I was walkin' a pair of horses up the lane when I saw the same woman. I said, "How are you?" and she said, "You've got some nice cabbages there; do you mind if I have one?" So I said "OK" and she said, "You won't let the bull out this time, will you?" Well, I had no idea she knew what happened the time before and I felt as small as anything.

HAYMAKING IDYLL

BANDS of mowers, in their light dresses and broad straw hats, are astir long before the fiery eye of the sun glances above the horizon, that they may toil in the freshness of the morning, and stretch themselves at noon in luxurious ease by trickling waters, and beneath the shade of trees. Till then, with regular strokes, and a sweeping sound, the sweet and flowery grass falls before them, revealing, at almost every step, nests of young birds, mice in their cosy domes, and the mossy cells of the humble-bee streaming with liquid honey: anon, troops of haymakers are abroad, tossing the green swaths to the sun. It is one of nature's festivities, endeared by a thousand pleasant memories and habits of the olden days, and not a soul can resist it. There is a sound of tinkling teams and waggons rolling along lanes and fields the whole country over, — ay, even at midnight, — till at length, the fragrant ricks rise in the farmyard, and the pale smooth-shaven fields are left in solitary beauty.

WILLIAM HOWITT, Book of the Seasons, 1830

'In those days we had a herd of about 25-30 Shorthorn; it was all Shorthorn then, but now it's all Friesian and you can't find a Shorthorn anywhere, but you get more milk from the Friesian. A cow used to cost about £10, perhaps £15 for an exceptional one. When father took on North Farm at the auction he only paid £100 for everything – cows, ol' plough, everythin'. We had a full-time cowman even though all the family helped with the milking.

'Also, in the summer we had to have help with the haymaking and then with pullin' up and trimmin' the mangels, which were stored behind the cowshed for cattle-feed. They were built up in a triangle and covered with straw; then we dug a trench round the bottom and earthed up over the straw to keep the straw on and the mangels dry. The cows always came in the first week in September; father was strict with that. They stayed in till the end of April, being fed hay and mangel and bedded on bracken.

'We used to go over to Holleycombe to cut the bracken by hand, at Sir John Hawkshaw's; he was our landlord and we had the right to it free. We brought it back in a waggon with a pair of horses. And we had another strip just down the road here at Redford. The bracken was put in a rick and thatched in, about the end of August.

'We had pigs too, about 20 breeding sows – mainly large whites. In the evening we'd let them out for the acorns and you wouldn't see them again till next morning; they used to wander miles. They were also fed our own mix of barley meal and crushed oats, all grown on the farm.

'One old field of ours had a stream runnin' through the middle and you couldn't do much with it, so we decided to cultivate with the old sows. We had this local carpenter – damn clever chap, could make

MARCH LAMBS

THE principal fall of lambs takes place now, and the shepherds are full of cares. Night and day they must be on the watch to assist the ewes, to cherish weakly lambs with warm milk, to restore others that appear dead by administering a little spirit; to counteract the unnatural disposition of some mothers that refuse their offspring; or to find foster-mothers for poor orphans, which is often done by clothing them in the skins of the dead lambs of those ewes to which they are consigned. Others for which no foster-mothers can be found, or which cannot suck on account of their being wry-necked, are reared generally by the assistance of a tea-pot with cow's milk, and are called cades or pets.

The shepherds of large flocks have a house built in a quadrangle, round which there are sheds where the ewes and their lambs can be sheltered and fed; and a fire is kept up day and night in the shepherd's lodge, to which any perishing or weakly lambs may be brought. Their contrivances also in the fields are various and interesting. The sheep are kept upon turnips, so as to maintain their strength and afford sufficient nourishment to the lambs; screens of hurdles, or straw, or fern, are raised to keep off the wind, and troughs with corn, and linseed-cake, are placed here and there in the fields where they feed, also furnished with screens of wood, hurdle, or other material, at once to protect the sheep as they feed and prevent the corn being blown out by the winds.

WILLIAM HOWITT
Book of the Seasons, 1830

anything – build a big shed for the pigs, 12ft wide and 24ft long. He made it in the yard and we took it down the field in sections it was so heavy. The carpenter suggested anchorage for it, but father said no – it was big and heavy, and in any case it was sheltered by the wood.

'Then one night we had an awful gale, and when I went down to feed next morning the sows were lyin' where the shed was, but the shed was away across the field more or less intact, only a board or two broken. Unfortunately, the wind had blown from an unexpected direction. So we had to take the shed to pieces again to move it back into place. But this time it was anchored down properly.

'We used to run a boar in the field with the sows all the time, and as soon as we saw one or two gettin' heavy, we'd shut them up at the farm and give them better food. Now and then one had eight, but mostly we had litters of ten; that was good then. But they were in good condition runnin' out all the time.

'Most of the pigs were sold live at market, but we also killed a few for home use. Every village 'ad a pig sticker then and it was a special day when he came, with a big staff on hand. We had to hold each pig on its back while he stuck the knife in its throat. That was one job I always hated – poor old pig squealin' away.

'The joints were salted down in big pottery containers and put in the cellar. Once a month mother went down and rubbed more salt in. They were big pigs we killed then, about five or six months old, not like the little squirts you get now.

'We used both Chichester and Petersfield markets. I was at Petersfield the day it closed – must have been 35 years ago. Chichester was on alternate Wednesdays to Petersfield; they had dairy cows, but Petersfield was mainly killing, except for calves. If you bought a cow at Chichester the only way to get it home, unless you had your own lorry – and they weren't much cop – was by rail. We'd put a cow and calf on the rail at Chichester and the head carter would take an ol' dung cart down to meet them at Midhurst. He'd load the calf aboard and the cow would follow the 6 miles home.

'We'd get down to Chichester for 9.30 and Petersfield for 10 am. There was a bar in the yard open all day, but I couldn't go in till I was 20. But I didn't want to anyway because of an earlier incident. After pheasant shooting had finished each year, each tenant farmer was allowed a day's rabbit shooting on his farm and we'd get about 20 Guns out. One day dad couldn't go and I went in his place. At lunchtime the hot water ran out for tea so I was tempted to take a glass of beer for the first time in my life. Unfortunately, it must have been off and when I went home that night I felt done in, so I went to bed early and later on I brought it all up. After that I never touched it for years.

'When we first started on the rabbit shoots we shot about 50, but then I started to soak strips of paper in Renodine and stuff them down the holes the day before. This kept the rabbits out and we got the bag up to about 150.

'We were very lucky in having the help of a one-armed dog man from Fernhurst. He had a lot of spaniels and terriers and the way those dogs obeyed him was remarkable. Those ol' dogs loved him, but he always asked us not to

bring any other dogs so that they wouldn't get distracted. He never charged us, but we always went round with a hat and he'd end up with a pound or so – that was a week's wages for most – of them.

'In those days we had an old Ford van – used to frighten me to death. No dashboard then, of course. There was a box by the steering-wheel and dad was always rooting around inside it to sort the ignition out – sparks flyin' everywhere. That must have been the late 1920s.

'Us boys used to like market days at Chichester because we always hoped to see Old Man Alley, who had the knacker-house at Liphook. As soon as we spotted him, we'd point him out to dad, who was always busy talking to someone else. But we'd keep on until we got them together for a word or two. The reason was that as soon as he shook hands with us in dropped 2s, a florin; he was always good to us boys.

'We had a lot of screw cows then. You couldn't sell 'em at market because they'd cock their tails up and out would come a stream of water – some sort of disease. But Old Man Alley always took them. One day I was up at his yard and asked his man where they all went. He said the boss took 'em up to London, to the East End, because the people up there were so poor they'd take anything.

'I don't know what dad got for those cows and it was a job to tell the prices paid at auction. At first I couldn't understand the auctioneer's gabber at all. The only time you' eard the price was when the hammer went down, and it would soon go up again if he heard another bid.

'The same man who made our pig-shed built the two houses for our 200 laying hens. The eggs used to go to market till the price went right down. Then a neighbour took some to sell around the big houses at Haslemere, where fresh farm eggs were so welcome he soon sold out. He did so well, the following week he had to take a pony and trap up, and after that he took our eggs for years.'

MARCH PLOUGHING

IN THE fields labourers are plashing and trimming the hedges, and in all directions are teams at plough. You smell the wholesome and, I may truly say, aromatic soil, as it is turned up to the sun, brown and rich, the whole country over. It is delightful, as you pass along deep hollow lanes, or are hidden in copses, to hear the tinkling gears of the horses, and the clear voices of the lads calling to them. It is not less pleasant to catch the busy caw of the rookery, and the first meek cry of the young lambs. The hares are hopping about the fields, the excitement of the season overcoming their habitual timidity. The bees are revelling in the yellow catkins of the sallow. The harmless English snake is seen again curled up, like a coil of rope, with its head in the centre, on sunny green banks.

WILLIAM HOWITT, Book of the Seasons, 1830

Ken became closely involved with horses when the carter was leaving 'and I took over his team. First day I went out he played a trick on me. We were going out to do some chain harrowing, to level out mole heaps on grassland. When he was backing the horses into place he deliberately twisted-the chains which fixed to the harrows on the side I couldn't see. Then he said, "See what you've done".

'The first time I went ploughing I was nearly finished come dinner-time. But when I saw father he said, "It's because plough is not set right: it should carry on up the field if you take your hands off the reins". He showed me how to set it properly. We had five horses – mainly Clydesdales and a shire. I loved ploughing.

'In the old days we only grew a few cereals – oats, which we crushed for the horses and cows, and barley ground for the pigs. Under the agreement with the landlord you only had certain fields under arable to supply your cattle and horses, but not for sale. So father was pleased when the War Agriculture ordered that a certain acreage of grass had to be ploughed up for corn. In those days he paid 10s an acre rent and we had about 125 acres.

'I used to plough all day long, from eight till five to get just an acre done. But there was always something to look at, and no noise.

'The first farm machines I can remember were the traction engines and thrashers. You hired the driver as well and he came out from Petersfield to do all the farms in the area as there was only a small quantity of cereals grown. He also towed his hut and elevator and the whole thing was like a circus coming along the road.

'I've also cut corn by hand, with a scythe about 4ft out from the hedge so the binder had a clear run and the horse wouldn't trample it down. There was no waste then; every bucketful was useful.

'We bought our first tractor, a Fordson, in 1932, when I came back from twelve months at Sparsholt Agricultural College. It was secondhand and comin' off the flints the tyres was nearly bare. Our binder was Massey Harris. Nowadays you only get the odd binder where they want wheatstraw for thatching as the combines chop it all up.'

Sheep, too, have figured prominently in Ken's life. Traditionally, local farmers had Kent store lambs up for the winter. They had to come off the marshes, where they would otherwise get bogged down, and Ken's farm could accommodate them well as there was a lot of autumn grass with the cows coming in early. They usually had about 60 up by train from Midhurst, 'but once we had to walk about 12 miles with them, back from Northchapel Station.

'There were always other flocks of sheep on the road then, but we never did get mixed up, even though it took most of the day to run them home. I used to fetch them with my dog in the early Thirties; he was the best I ever had. One day when I got down to Midhurst to collect the sheep the agent said, "Where's your men?" – all the others had half-a-dozen. He was quite worried about it. But I said, "Don't you fret, Bob'll keep 'em apart". So they unloaded the lot and away we went – me walking in front all the way and the dog behind. After a while we came up to a big flock with six men and two of their sheep came back, but Bob soon cut 'em out, and the same happened with a flock behind.

'I always remember this chap came hurtling down the hill on a bike with no brakes. I shouted at him but 'e smacked into the bank and rolled back down on the sheep.

'We used to have the sheep from the end of September till the

end of February or early March. At first the owner used to pay us
about 3d a week per sheep, but the last lot we had was 6d. Whole
trainloads came into the area then. You had to have good fences to
keep them in as they were used to roaming over much larger areas
on the marshes. They didn't take a lot of looking after really. Just
a bit of hay all loose then, no bales – if it was snowy. You had to
watch for foot-rot though, any cases being trimmed out and a mix of
Stockholm tar and salt being put on. After we had the lambs, they
went back to Kent for fattening on grass and selling.

'Once we had the sheep on the golf course up at Holleycombe. On
Boxing Day I used to go up to feed them first before going on to a
shoot at my wife's parents' farm at Lurgashall. But one Christmas
I went, I had the biggest shock of my life. There were sheep lyin' all
over the place and I had to kill six with my knife, they were mauled
so badly. And wool! – you've never seen anythin' like it. I rang the
police, but they never found the culprits; they thought there was
a pack of dogs gone wild. It was the only time I ever had sheep
worrying, but it upset me so much I never had any more sheep there.

'When Sir John Hawkshaw died, father wanted to buy his farm
of 125 acres, but the executors said the whole estate had to be sold
in one lot. And farms were cheap
then, too. So then I decided to
start up here, at Woolbeding,
in 1942.

'Farming was a reserved
occupation, of course, but I
did sign on for the Air Force.
In the end I volunteered for
the Home Guard and we

used to be on duty up here at the Duchess of Bedford's hangar. She used to fly a plane but was killed.

'One winter night I was in charge and there used to be two of us on duty and four sleepin'. But it was too cold in the hangar, so we moved into the cottage alongside. We went up at 9 pm and my younger brother Cecil was with me. He was a good cook and we decided to have a good cook-up. But first we went off to Midhurst in the car for a drink and to bring back some beer. There we met two girls we knew in the pub and invited them back for a meal.

'We'd just finished our cook-up when a chap came runnin' in to say that the commanding officer had just arrived, so one girl slid under a bed and the other went in a cupboard. Fortunately, the CO was quite a lad. In he came and said, "You've got a good sentry there – well done. And that's a fine smell. Been cooking? "Then he settled down and started to tell us such a good yarn the girls started gigglin' and he heard them. So out they had to come and he said, "What's two lovely girls like you doin' in there? I wish I'd known you were there before." After that, we all had a nice evening together and the CO even took the girls home.

'It was very tiring then; after all night on duty I had to go home, milk the cows and then go haymakin' all day. There was never any set hours; if the weather was right you had to get on with it. Haymakin' was a lot of hard work – all by hand then, but some people had a horse rake, going round clearing up what you missed with a prong.

'When I first took this farm I didn't live here. I was very lucky because there were four land girls workin' here on the thrashin'. They were supplied by the War Agriculture; it was an alternative to going in the forces. And when it was wet and we couldn't thrash,

they came up here and scrubbed out and painted the rooms, so we had a lovely start. I only had pigs here then.

'But when I came up one evening I was confronted by a sentry, who called "Halt!" I said, "What you doin' here?"

and he said, "It's been taken over". "No", I said, "it's my house; you can't do that". So I called for the CO and he said it had been taken over as there was no one living there. But he let me through and I went to the barn where I had 2 ton of seed potatoes stored. Well, the soldiers had their kit all over 'em and were layin' across the sacks. So I soon said they'll have to get off and sleep on the floor.

'After that first day they were quite nice and let me come and go. They stayed about a week, but you daren't ask them where they came from or where they were going. They was all gettin' ready for the second front then.'

In the following year, 1943, Ken got married; his wife died in 1979. They had three children and now their son runs the little 75-acre farm. There are a few sheep, but the main concern is the riding stable, in the care of Ken's daughter-in-law. His son also works on other farms.

Fit for his age, Ken still drives the tractor a bit and manages occasional fencing work. He is obviously a restless spirit and seems ill at ease in the peaceful atmosphere of his black-beamed living-room, where only the gentle tick of a Horsham-made grandfather clock breaks the silence when his toddler granddaughter is not there climbing all over him.

Ken's great energy is obviously inherited. 'Grandfather went out on his 81st birthday to see what he could kill with 25 cartridges. He shot while another man worked the ferrets and he came back with a pigeon and 25 rabbits – two came out one hole together! He was delighted. This was down on Pitt Farm, Cadbury, Devon, and I was so pleased I was down there then; he died the following year.'

In earlier years, Ken once went down to Devon for a holiday, travelling pillion on his brother's BSA motorbike. 'We pulled into this petrol station – single pump with rotary winder – and this proper Devon bloke said, "You be foreigners". We said, "No we're not", and he said, "You don't come from Devon". That must have been in the late Twenties.'

But the fact is that Ken is of the type who could never be called a 'foreigner' in any county. Dig gently beneath that facade of an accent to find the true character of the countryside, that good yeoman stock whose line is apparently endless. He may have been on local television and on the BBC's Songs of Praise, but his abiding place is as a pillar of village life. Not for nothing has he been a churchwarden for over 35 years.

After Ken died in October 2002, aged 86, his son Martin, who was born at Pound Farm, took over but had to sell up when the lease expired in 2008.

FREE SPIRIT

Bill Thompson, Hurdle-maker

As A young man, Bill Thomson seemed destined to endure the drudge of farm labouring, but in the end his refusal to accept subservience secured a job which gave him the independence he has always cherished. 'I got fed up with milkin' some farmer's cows on a Sunday afternoon and I didn't like the attitude of the farmer to the farm worker, which still prevails to this day in some places, though things are much improved.

'Don't get me wrong – I like farming, but not farm work. In the last century my family were farmers in Lanarkshire, but with the depression after World War I my paternal grandfather went bankrupt and was obliged to take work, so he came south. Father followed in his footsteps with general farm work, mainly shepherding, and I was born at St Neots, Huntingdonshire (now Cambridgeshire) on 31 December 1935. I was christened William Ian, there being a Will Thomson in the family since the 1800s.

'I didn't like school and always preferred the open air. But I've always been a great reader and my ambitions came a bit too late. Really I'd like to have been a vet. But in my day in a rural secondary modern school you were simply turned out with sufficient skill to work on a farm, in the woods or some other trade; you never had any grounding for a profession.

'I left school at 14 – it should have been 15, but with my birthday falling the way it did I was let out a bit early. After school then people tended to kick about in a few jobs because you knew you were going in the Army anyway. Incidentally, I volunteered in 1954 because I would have been conscripted for three years and the Thomsons have always volunteered. Anyway, it meant I got £1 a week more than I'd been earning. I was in Tripoli, Libya, for over two years.'

On the farm, Bill had earned about £3 a week with overtime, but had a 5-mile bike ride before he started work at 6 am each morning. It was thankless work and he was pleased to take up forestry when he was 17.

After leaving the Army in 1957, he had no job to go to and, 'after being freed from the constraints of service life I naturally wanted to have a good time for a few months. Then I started with a timber-felling gang at Coldharbour for two years. Earning £10 a week I was a lord, but it was very hard- piece-work. This was one of the first jobs where people worked only five days a week and we earned about five bob an hour. With 6lb axe and cross-cut saw, we felled the timber and trimmed it out for about 5d a cube.

'To stack a cord of wood we earned 16s. The reason why the old inglenook fireplace was that size was because they could put the cordwood straight on – they didn't have the machinery to cut it up easily in the old days.

'Being on piece-work, the men used to get up to all sorts of tricks when stacking, such as laying the timber all over a stump. The old foreman used to come along and say, "I don't mind seeing a hole a fox can run through, but not one where the hounds can chase after him". Yes, there were lots of stories about slack stacks.

'We went all over the place, mostly in Surrey, Sussex and Hampshire. I was young and fit then and could work with the best of 'em, but even that wasn't good enough sometimes, so I was even more keen to get my independence. There was no hurdle-making in the area then – only peasticks and beansticks. The copse cuttin' all stopped in the spring, so we needed to do something else in the summer and I wanted a job to last all year.

'Anyway, I was working down near Alton, in Hampshire, and comin' home one night had to take a diversion which, by chance, took me out to the back of beyond. There I came across this ol' boy hurdle-making and this really fired my imagination as I'd been thinking about it for some time anyway.

'Then one Saturday afternoon in Smith's – I was always in some bookshop or other – I came across this book on woodland crafts, by Edland. In this the author acknowledged the help of the Rural Industries Bureau, so I wrote to them at Wimbledon and asked if there was someone who could show me the craft. Then their local man came out to see me and they fixed for me to go down to Hampshire for instruction by an old man. There was no charge for the instruction, but it would cost me about £20 to take the two weeks off work, and then there was about £10 for the lodgin'. Some of the old chaps I knew were appalled; they said, "You'll never get your money back". And that was in 1959. God knows what they'd have been like in the real old days – a lot of 'em never want to see you get on.

'Even that old boy suffered a bit because he was one of the few willing to teach people and therefore increase the competition. He's still disliked in the area today. He lived in the village of Crawley, near King's Somborne, and worked on Lord and Lady Docker's estate. His memory went way back and he told me how in the Great War a lot of them had contracts to make hurdles to shore up the

trenches. But they've been used in warfare for hundreds of years.

'For the first week with the old hurdle-maker, I lodged in Stockbridge, but I got so little to eat I told the ol' boy and he fixed me up with a neighbour. Fortunately, because I'd worked with coppice and was well used to the tools, I got on well and the ol' chap did pay me the compliment of saying he'd never seen anyone pick it up so quick. Starting green as grass would take you a long time; it's taken me three years to train my partner.

'My teacher was just like something out of Thomas Hardy; he used to go round and pay his five or six men with money taken out of an old string bag. Hurdle-making was a very old established trade in Hampshire and as well as the makers there used to be men whose job it was simply to go round and cut a 'score' of copse, which was enough for each man, and he had to do it in a day before moving on to the next. Some of them also had a horse and cart to get the hurdles out to a road where a lorry could pick them up. But they never made hurdles.'

After finishing his course, Bill, who was still single, went back to his lodgings at South Holmwood, in Surrey, and from then on was a full-time hurdle-maker.

'I'd already been cutting hazel for bean and pea boughs and I soon destroyed the myth up here that if you cut hazel in the summer it would die. Now I could work all the year round and I had my true independence. Straight away I rang some of the wood merchants, who I'd been doin' business with anyway, and one said to me, "Boy, you done the right thing – they'll always be wanted".

'The big problem then was gettin' the right quality copse – we call it underwood as opposed to the actual timber. I was only a lad really and just imagine, I had to go and knock on some farmer's door only to be told, "No, old so and so's had that copse for years, but there is a rough ol' bit you can 'ave". Nowadays I'm all right though, as all the old boys are dead and I get first choice!

'At first my customers were mainly small wood merchants who moved the hurdles on. This was always a source of irritation to me as I wanted to do away with the middle men. Unfortunately, there wasn't much I could do about it till I was married and had my own house and phone and could advertise.'

SPRINGTIME HAZE

In spring the ground here is hidden by a verdant growth, out of which presently the anemone lifts its chaste flower. Then the wild hyacinths hang their blue bells so thickly that, glancing between the poles, it is hazy with colour; and in the evening, if the level beams of the red sun can reach them, hare and there a streak of imperial purple plays upon the azure. Woodbine coils round the tall straight poles, and wild hops, whose bloom emits a pleasant smell if crushed in the fingers.

On the upper and clearer branches of the hawthorn the nightingale sings – more sweetly, I think, in the freshness of the morning than at night. Resting quietly on an ash-stole, with the scent of flowers, and the odour of green buds and leaves, a ray of sunlight yonder lighting up the lichen and the moss on the oak trunk, a gentle air stirring in the branches above, giving glimpses of fleecy clouds sailing in the ether, there comes into the mind a feeling of intense joy in the simple fact of living.

RICHARD JEFFRIES
Wild Life in a Southern County, 1879

Bill has concentrated on making hurdles far garden screens and windbreaks and has never made any of the fold hurdles which were the mainstay of downland sheep country. The shepherd's hurdles always had a gap called a twilly, which enabled him to put his crook through and carry several over his shoulder. But occasionally Bill is called upon to make a few specials, such as those for penning pet sheep, to hide unsightly oil-tanks in the countryside, and once even to act as a weir in a river.

The standard hurdle is 6ft square and almost entirely of hazel, 'unless there are other bits of wood in the copse. Hazel's the only wood that splits and weaves nicely. I wouldn't go lookin' for willow. I charge about £24 for a hurdle, but my ol' teacher said to me, "You want to charge 17s 6d for one of those big ones, boy!". However, when I came back I thought there's no hurdle-maker up here, so I'll-try 19s.

'The landscapers like hurdles as they're easy to put up, and they're good news with all the gales we've been having as they have a bit of movement in them and the wind blows right through. We were really busy after the Great Storm of 1987. Once I was asked to make 200 for the sheep fair at Finden, in Sussex, but I couldn't manage to do all of them in time so I asked an ol' boy in Dorset to make 100. He asked me if I wanted twillies, but I very soon said no as they'd be sold off after, as windbreaks.

'Some people ask me if the work is monotonous, but I say there's never two hurdles been made the same. Every hurdle you're fightin' with it, you've got to let it know who's the boss. But it's the continuity I like best. Some of the copses are hundreds of years old and I like to think of all the old boys who've been working at each stump. Sometimes it's quite eerie; where we are now I know at least three men dead who used to cut it. William Cobbett (author of *Rural Rides*, 1830) rode past here and he would have known what we're doing.

'Another thing that adds a lot of interest is the wildlife; it helps make your day – same as the change in the seasons. There's always something to see, even if it's only the mice we chuck bread out for at dinner-time. Mind you, I think some of these wildlife people have gone overboard. Now they're all very keen to have the derelict copses cut and are pleased to have you in because it helps the wildlife, but some of them haven't got a clue. One wildlife officer even asked me to leave a bough arched across a path so that the dormice could run over it. I said, "What's wrong with the ground? They've been using it for millions of years". In the old days, when there was far more wildlife around than there is now, the old standard was to burn all the rubbish and leave a copse so clean you could see a mouse runnin' about. With good copse management the wildlife will always thrive and there's nothing we'd do to hurt it.

'The National Trust has been very good to me and I've worked mainly in the Leith Hill area, in Surrey. Where I am now I've cut three times and I hope to cut it once more before I pack up. We're restoring a lot, too, The Trust supplies me with plants in the winter and I fill in the gaps as I go around. It's essential to work on rotation. In my younger days it was much more haphazard, you cut a piece one year and the next a farmer put his pigs out and destroyed it.

'We generally use eight-year-old hazel, sometimes seven. It's best south-facing and fairly well drained, especially by a brook. Walk through a copse on flat land and you'll see where they dug ditches out to get the growth. The quality varies a lot and we almost used to fight over it. Down in Hampshire it was auctioned standing and they used to get up to all sorts of tricks such as swapping the lot numbers around. The trade was never that strong up here – it was always tied up with downs and sheep.

Woven hurdles or fences not only look attractive but are probably the oldest form of fencing in Britain, dating back to Neolithic times. Robust, beautiful and organic, they blend into the landscape and their materials, harvested from sustainable woodlands, are renewable. Of the woods available, hazel and willow, because they are so supple, are still the best and most popular ones to choose. The centre for Alternative Technology (www2.cat.org.uk) provides detailed information on obtaining, making and using traditional hurdles. Or at www.allotmentforestry.com you can find step-by-step instructions for making your own. This site also contains details of The Local Woodland Products Initiative, whose aim it IS to increase the use of sustainable woodland products in the garden.

Nationally, Britain still has around 150 specialist hurdle makers, but the future of hurdle-making is threatened by shortages of quality raw material, by the older workers being unwilling to take on apprentices, and by the shortage of training programmes. Equally, outside southern England, hazel coppice is in short supply; as a result large quantities of are now imported, mainly from Eastern Europe.

'You've got to love the job to be up there in all weathers. The only thing that drives you home is when you run out of tea. I've had my sandwiches frozen in my box before now. I've never been out of work since I got established, but the demand is seasonal, so you must have a little money behind you to tide you over. The winter order is always down so I generally sell a few logs, too. Although we make up, stack and sort the wood into sizes all the year round you have to stop work with the light as workin' with edge tools is dangerous. Mind you, in my younger days we made by lantern to get the money. I've cut both knees with a billhook in my time, though once was the fault of a rabbit really. Where he'd gnawed around a stump the wood wouldn't split easily, so I gave it an extra thump and sliced myself too. Other times it's familiarity breeds contempt. I remember an old tree haulier who broke the rules even though he'd worked in the woods all his life, so a big tree rolled over and killed him.

'Another thing I suffer with is bad hands – they split all the time in frosty weather, even though I often wear gloves as well as leather knee-pads. In winter you can't work fast enough to keep warm. We have a fire by us and a kind of hut made from a few old hurdles; and we both take our dogs up for company.

'A man working in a craft such as this really needs to have his wits about him as well as being skilled. You've got to be a bit of a businessman; when I look at my bank statement there seems to be more direct debits than there are cheques drawn. And even though we now

use a chainsaw, you're really in a job you can't mechanise. My only real tools are billhooks – I have four old ones I've picked up along the way – and a stone to sharpen them. Nowadays it's rare for us to cut with the hook. They used to say you'll kill the hazel with the chainsaw. You still hear it now; some people are so rigid and have a fixed idea of you and
your work.

'With your hands you can only get the rods [cross pieces] so tight, so every three or so we give a clump with a wooden maul. The hurdles must be as tight and as square as possible, especially if you're putting 'em up! They're made on a slight curve as a form of tensioning. When they dry out they go flat but still keep tight. If you made them flat they'd fall apart when dry. I often wonder how some old boy discovered that.

'The other thing people always ask me is how long do they last. Well, it's according to the site as they go on more where it's sheltered. If I put them up on my own chestnut stakes, then eight to ten years is a good average. But you know how people are always keen to save money and sometimes good hurdles are ruined by a bit of DIY and rubbish posts. Some of the very oldest hurdles have been used inside buildings to separate livestock, and those used with wattle and daub in walls are often centuries old. They were used back in Neolithic times to keep the soil out of grain pits, but the very oldest hurdling ever found is 5,000 years old and comes from the Somerset Levels. It was made of hazel and willow and laid down flat to act as a walkway where they drove cattle through the marshes. It was preserved in the peat and we can see that they did not have metal tools to work with because the rods are round and not split.

'Hazel is a wonderful crop with no enemies and no diseases; it's God's greatest gift to the rural economy. As long as it's regularly cut it Will go on indefinitely. Of course, hurdle-makers don't want any big trees in a wood, apart from a few for summer shade, but there's a lot to be said for the old system of coppice with standards. When we had the hurricane there were hardly any oaks down where they were surrounded by hazel copse, but where there was no coppice they went down like dominoes, even on the same estate.

'Round here the big trade up to the 1930s in coppice was in hoop shavin' for slack cooperage such as sugar-casks, which were not actually watertight. But hazel strips were also bound around beer-barrels to protect them as they were rolled along.

'There were still a lot of pea and bean sticks and faggots being cut up to the late 1950s. Many, many thousands were cut and big

dealers used to take them up to the London suburbs. The pea sticks finished when pick-your-own vegetables came in, as well as the weight restrictions on lorries; in the old days they were loaded up as high as you could lift 'em. I saw the trade petering out and that was one reason why I went into hurdle-making.

'The demand for faggots was tremendous. I remember the baker at Alfold permanently had a pile there as big as a hayrick. All the brickworks used faggots, too. Lots of copses have old names to do with brickworks, such as Kiln Copse. The faggots were bundles of brushwood as wide as a steering-wheel and 4ft long, but there were different sorts and bakers had smaller ones for their bread ovens.

'So altogether there was no waste at all in the wood. Some of the old boys would be horrified if they came back now – we burn everything you can't make a hurdle out of. But there was a lot of cheap labour in their day. Farmers laid off no end of people in the winter and at first the brickyards generally only made bricks in the summer.'

One thing that Bill obviously regrets is how attitudes to jobs have changed, in that younger people are less inclined to take pride in their work. 'There must be willingness as well as skill. It's all too quick now. Do you know, there's a college which actually runs one-day courses in hurdle-making; would you believe it? The skill can never be written down.

'Another thing that's changed is people's attitude at country shows; there's always somebody that makes a nuisance of himself. One year at Ardingly, the South of England show, this ol' boy was a bit impertinent and a pest. Next year he was the same and eventually came up and, not remembering me, said, "Well, you're not makin' a bad job of it, but you're not quite as good as the bloke who was here last year".

Some of Bill's customers can be odd, too. 'There was one notorious ol' local woman who we were buildin' a dog run for and she never gave anyone anythin' if she could help it. Well, blow me if one day out she came with what seemed to be something for me. But no, she handed me a plate of chocolate biscuits and said, "Thomson, take these, and if I'm not back by 12 give them to the dogs". Needless to say, as soon as she'd gone I ate them.

'We've had some strange encounters in the woods, too. Over at Alfold once there was a continuous stream of couples going down the path with blankets under their arms. We used to speculate how so many people managed to get time off in the daytime.'

Now Bill lives alone in some comfort in a modern bungalow, on an estate at Ewhurst, near Cranleigh, his two daughters having grown up and moved away. He has invested wisely and held a smallholding of about 3 acres from 1972 to 1986. Yet he remembers vividly the hard times, such as in the freeze-up of early 1963, when he had barely two halfpennies to rub together. And the years of hard work have taken their toll on his body, with the usual hurdle-maker's history of back trouble. 'In the old days, when we worked right down on the ground, sometimes I had to pull myself up by the hurdles, but raising the work up mostly cured it.' And then there were the years of piece-work which would have taken many lesser men to an early grave.

Although hopefully still with many good years before him, Bill is already content in having achieved his three goals. 'I always wanted to leave the woods in better condition than when I found them, to make a living from it, and to pass on what I've learned to someone else.' At a 'mere' 56 years old, Bill might be the youngest person in this book, but he is a true free spirit and among the greatest champions of the old ways.

Bill Thomson died in 2002, aged 67.

HARDY PERENNIAL

George Ayling, Nurseryman

At 86 years old and still working, nurseryman George ('Digger') Ayling puts his good health down to honest toil. 'I was born in 1906, on 19 March – St Joseph's Day – and as he's the patron saint of workers, I suppose I have to keep going.'

Yet George's longevity is both surprising and lucky. For a start, both his father and grandfather died suddenly at the age of 63. His postman grandfather died of a brain haemorrhage when he was emptying the letterbox at the Sussex village of Lodsworth, and his father succumbed to a heart attack in 1945. 'Father was brought home and we did get Dr Bailey to give him an injection. In the afternoon he gradually became worse but we could not get a doctor anywhere. I got the local nurse, but she could not save him.'

Furthermore, when George was 55 he had such a lucky escape that it made news in the local paper. It was on a freezing mid-April night in 1961, at about 10.30pm, when George went down to tend a boiler in his greenhouses. Concerned for his plants, he increased the oil fuel supply to provide more hot water to help his charges survive. But when the fuel vapour poured into the combustion chamber the electric ignition system failed to work.

George realised what would happen and dived for the off switch, but he was too late. The vapour exploded on the hot walls of the chamber, blasting open the massive iron doors. He ducked instinctively, but it was predominantly luck that saved him from instant death. The explosion shook doors and windows a quarter of a mile away, blew off the glass roof of the boiler-house and smashed a lot of glass in the greenhouse. 'The neighbours thought it was a bomb!'

At first, George thought he had been blinded by the blast, but as he staggered outside, his hair singed off and blood streaming down his face, he realised that his glasses had been completely blackened by the soot. 'I snatched them off and could see the stars as clear as you. By golly, I really did think there was a God up there lookin' down on me. You can't imagine how relieved I was.'

Nonetheless, most of the skin on George's face was seared off. 'But when the doctor saw me all she could do was laugh. "I'm sorry", she said, "but you look so funny all black, no hair and bleeding." After hospital treatment they sent me home, swathed in bandages.

'Next day we picked up three wheelbarrowfuls of glass – it was stuck in all over the place, even in the door frame next to where I stood. And the poor old cat had followed me down too. He was hit all right, but survived; then, he was a black cat! As for me, well, they used to say that you were lucky if a 2s piece could be passed through the gap in your teeth. Just look at mine – you could get two in there, so it's no wonder I survived.'

George William Ayling was born and grew up in the delightful Sussex countryside on and around the South Downs, near Midhurst. His father was a gardener and the family lived at Lodsworth and Steyning before they settled at Singleton, where George started school at the age of 3½. 'Father worked for the Reverend Horden and we lived in one of a pair of cottages by the rectory.'

One of George's earliest memories is of when he was playing in the road and his mother called him in to tell him that the king had died. In those days Edward VII was a regular guest at West Dean, where he enjoyed the shooting parties, and one of the king's detectives – Inspector Rule of Scotland Yard – used to lodge with the Aylings.

Unfortunately, when Reverend Horden was replaced, the new incumbent brought his own gardener and George's father was made redundant. He decided therefore to start up on his own and rented 2½ acres from the Piggot family at nearby Ingram's Green. 'He borrowed £100 from his sister and took 20 years to pay it back.'

Ayling, senior started to grow outdoor vegetables plus tomatoes, cucumbers and' melons in the glasshouse. George can just remember that the summer of 1911 was hot enough to grow melons in a cold frame. 'But these were tough times and we were bloomin' hard up for much of the time. One day mother was crying 'cos we only had wood for the stove, so I went up to Elsted Station with 2s from my money-box to buy her a bag of coal. But everybody was hard up then and we never put coal on the fire after about 7pm. Our lighting was candles and paraffin lamps and we had to save every bit we could.

'We used to keep a few pigs and chickens. Mother used to pick and draw the birds and we sold the eggs. I always remember that two of the girls who used to come up for eggs – Captain Leveson's parlour maid and house maid – went down on the Titanic when they were emigrating.

'With the pigs, a butcher used to come in and slit their throats and scald the hair off. They'd be cut up, the joints rubbed in saltpetre, flesh in salt, covered in sacking and hung up on the hooks in the big old chimney of our 1737 house. Damn nice bacon it was too, nothing like it nowadays. But one day dad had to sell the old sow and some piglets to pay the miller's bill – and he was an Ayling! There was never much meat in those days and whenever he could dad would catch a rabbit, or shoot one with his little .22 rifle. That was a treat. Also, once or twice he had a pheasant out of the apple tree, but he had to watch it, though, as it was a rented house.

'We used to take our water straight from the stream and the water rats used to scurry away when I went down with the bucket. Sometimes the water was all chalky where the cows had paddled in it upstream, but we never used to mind and drank it as soon as it settled in the bucket.

'Things were very different then; everything was done by horses. About 8 in the morning all the milk-carts would be coming along in all directions, making their way to Elsted Station, and then there was another lot of churns at 5 pm. And there was a horse and waggon which used to take blotting-paper up to the station and came back with the rags to make another lot at Iping Mill, which was burnt down in October, 1924.

'They were tough times all right and there was some pretty tough men about. Cor, I remember old Waxy West at the local saw-pit – darn great strong chap he was. But we had a bit of fun, too. Most of the time all us kids had was a tennis ball to kick about like a football, but when I was 8 I did get a secondhand bike for 7s 6d, even though it was a girl's model. And I used to enjoy climbing up Mrs Neville's dovecote at Trotton Place. It was built in 1626, had 1,200 nestboxes and a pair of white owls lived there.

GARDEN PARADISE

COTTAGE gardens are now perfect paradises; and, after gazing on their sunny quietude, their lilachs, peonies, wall-flowers, tulips, anemones and corcoruses with their yellow tufts of flowers, now becoming as common at the doors of cottages as the rosemary and rue once were — one cannot help regretting that more of our labouring classes do not enjoy the freshness of earth, and the pure breeze of heaven, in these little rural retreats, instead of being buried in close and sombre alleys. A man who can, in addition to a tolerable remuneration for the labour of his hands, enjoy a clean cottage and a garden amidst the common but precious offerings of Nature, the grateful shade of trees and the flow of waters, a pure atmosphere and a riant sky, can scarcely be called poor.

WILLIAM HOWITT
Book of the Seasons, 1830

first airship I saw was in 1913; it was the same shape as a Zeppelin. And I saw the R34 several times, as well as the Graf Zeppelin. Lots of balloons used to come over then. One day at Ingram's Green a chap called down, "Where are we?" He had his rope trailing with the anchor ready to drop down, and everybody was following him along. Eventually they came down with a bump at Didling. One chap broke his leg and a local farmer provided a waggon and horse to put the whole lot on the train at Elsted. That was during the Great War.

'I can still remember the assassination of the archduke and the outbreak of war; it was August Bank Holiday 1914, and father didn't have to go because he was producing vegetables and classified as a reserved occupation. But he did join the Derby Group, the 1914 Home Guard.

'One afternoon during the war we were let out of school early to watch 5,000 troops marching by. There were no lorries, only horses bringing the goods along, and they were all on their way to Dover.

'Then there was a very hard winter during the war and the stream froze so we could run all over it. And in 1916 the Daylight Saving Act was introduced. That humbugged some things up – fooled the cows, too. When she was a girl, mother used to take in washing for the man who brought it in. He's dead now, of course; they're all gone.'

George did well at Stedham School, but did not stay on until the customary leaving age of 14. When he was 12 he passed the Labour Examination and left to help his father for 6d a week. 'Grandfather left school at seven, but even in my day everyone started work by 7am and then worked till dark.

'It was all growing and selling vegetables and all father, had was a one-wheel truck.

'We used to go round and knock on people's doors. Unfortunately, the only tarred road was the main one from Petersfield to Midhurst, but in the 1920s they started to tar the others. I can still remember all the gravel and rock and chaps at the side of the road breaking it up with hammers.

'There were no punnets like there are now. Father used to get empty chocolate-boxes from a shop in Midhurst, line them with a cabbage leaf and put a pound of strawberries in. Peas, potatoes and apples were all sold by the gallon, but everyone knew exactly what they were getting.

'I knew a Mr Holden at Midhurst, who could remember when a car was only allowed to do 5mph because someone had to run along with a red flag in front. The first tradesman in the area to get a van was John Fish, the Midhurst butcher. Evans-Wild used to bring our bread out on a cart from Harting. Everyone used to have at least two or three loaves – it was hardly worth coming round for one.

'At first there were very few cars about, and they all belonged to rich or important people, such as Queen Mary who, after Goodwood, always used to call in to look at Miss Slade's antiques, by the Spread Eagle in Midhurst, on her way to Uppark at Harting.'

There were no telephones in the district until 1913, and although there was a small one at Stedham in 1921, there was no proper bus service before that of Southdown in 1922. These were motorised, but George can also remember seeing horse-drawn buses run by Thomas Tilling at Brighton.

TRAPPED FOR THE POT

WOODPIGEONS are killed in great numbers on cabbage and turnip-fields by day; in the neighbourhood of large woods, where they abound, the farmers' boys set steel-traps for them in the snow, laying a cabbage-leaf on each trap, to which they fly eagerly, and are abundantly captured; and by moonlight they are shot in the trees where they roost. Larks frequent the stubbles in vast flocks, and are destroyed by gun or net. Immense numbers of these delightful songsters are sent, during the winter months, from the neighbourhood of Dunstable to London, and may be seen by basketsfull at the poulterers'. They are in season from Michaelmas to February; and are not only served up at the inns in that town, by a secret process of cookery, in such a manner as to be regarded by travellers as a peculiar luxury, but are thence sent, by a particular contrivance of package, ready dressed to all parts of England.

The Dunstable people have what is called a larking-glass, which is fixed on a pole and twirled, and the larks come darting down to it in great numbers, and a net is drawn over them. Besides great quantities being thus taken, and also morning and evening with trammelling nets, others in severe weather are taken by laying a train of corn and chaff in the snow, and placing along it a line to which is fastened, at certain intervals, nooses of horse-hair, in which their feet are entangled.

WILLIAM HOWITT
Book of the Seasons, 1830

In 1924 the Aylings bought their first car for £45, from a butcher at Petersfield. 'It was a Swift, with just one gas carbide headlamp, oil side and rear lamps, spare wheel on the running board, a hood and a starting handle, but no windscreen wipers. Spotty Reece taught us to drive. I used 2 gallons on side roads and then Spotty said "You'll be all right now." I've never passed a driving test in my life. Just after the car I acquired my first motorbike – a single-speed Levis from Tew at Petersfield. Nowadays I don't drive much, usually only from home at Midhurst to the nursery and into Petersfield.'

In 1934 George, his father, and brother Wilfred took on just '3 acres of rough old grass' which is now the site of the successful 30-acre Ayling nursery at Trotton, on the Petersfield-Midhurst road. 'Lorna Baron wanted £300 for the land but we only had £75. But she let us put £25 down and pay the rest off in £25s over the next three years.

'When we started here we got a chap in to do a bit of ploughing, but most of it we dug by hand. It was all sand and very stony, but we just kept on putting in manure, then later put up the little wooden-sided glasshouses. Then the Woolwich lent us £600 to build a house, and in the late 1930s it cost just £7 10s to wire it. When I got married in 1938 I was only earning 2s 6d a week and it cost £120 to furnish the whole house.'

By that time George had taken up his father's keen interest in politics and even on the day after his wedding he was in the House of Commons listening to a debate. Indeed, when he was just 18 he was secretary of the Young Conservatives (then the Junior Imperial League) at Midhurst. 'But the biggest meeting I ever addressed was the Conservative Party Conference at Great Yarmouth in 1929. I'd sent in an amendment to do with agriculture and when I'd heard nothing I went round to see the big wigs at the Queen's Hotel. It was to do with the Merchandise Marks Act and we were all angry about tomatoes being labelled as English when they were foreign. In the end I got my say, and after the conference Colonel John Gretton said, "Why don't you take up politics as a profession?"'

But George resisted the lure of the soapbox and confined his politics to amateur interest. However, he has never been slow to put his point of view across, and in so doing has met a wide range of public figures, including Lord Haw Haw (William Joyce), who was attending a Fascist meeting at the Swan Hotel, Petworth, supporting Edward VIII in his marriage to American and commoner

Wallis Simpson. He even wrote to Mussolini to congratulate him on draining the Pontine Marshes with relatively little resources, and the reply he received is one of his greatest treasures. But I suspect that the high-point of all his politicising was when he met Margaret Thatcher at a Small Business Association meeting, just before she became Prime Minister.

When World War II broke out the Aylings were again saved from being called up because of their reserved occupation, but George joined the Home Guard. 'I was on duty when the first bombs were dropped round here and I could show you where every one fell.'

One wartime incident is especially vivid in George's memory: 'Early one August morning in 1940, I was at our Trotton nursery with a friend, watching an air battle. Between 7.30 am and 7.45 am we saw a plane shot down, with smoke billowing behind it. That evening my brother and I went into Elsted and down the road to Treyford. We then went up a grass track up into the woods opposite Elsted village. On the downs there were quite a few other people looking at a large, deep crater, from which smoke was still coming. There was a very nasty smell of burning flesh, which we were told was the German officer pilot burning. Some boys were poking about and one of them said: "Look, there's a bit of 'im." I said, "Don't do that; he might be the enemy, but he's some mother's son." It was very sad. Earlier in the day the first people on the scene saw a dog run off with a charred and smouldering human foot and leg.' George has since met the pilot's niece and her husband at the memorial stone.

In 1946 the Aylings acquired their first television set. 'It was a little 9in model and the man in the shop said we didn't need a licence because we were right on the boundary of where the Crystal Palace transmitter could reach and the signal was too weak. But he was wrong and in due course an official called to tell us so!'

The following winter was the coldest this century, apart from 1962–3. 'There was 34 degrees of frost and all our bloomin' stuff froze up. We only had little coke boilers and every night I had to come down at 10.30 to stoke 'em up before I went to bed, and I was back again at 3 am to shovel more on.'

The water supply used to be a special problem at Trotton. For a long time the nearest was at Midhurst or Petersfield, so it had to be obtained from the pond opposite the nursery. George can remember that as far back as 1912 the people there had to draw water by bucket and drag it back across the road. 'But there was no traffic then. In due course we had a well sunk, but there was only a hand-pump and it was not till electricity was put in that things got easier. There was a problem when the road was improved and part of the pond was filled in – after I had gone to so much trouble clearing it out! – but I persuaded the authorities to dig me another. Now we are on the mains.'

Mechanisation also made a big difference at the nursery. 'Our first bit of machinery was a rotavator, and after the war we had a Ferguson tractor. But today there are different needs as the vegetable market has gone in the face of cheap foreign imports and much of the land is down to pasture again as the concentration is on selling plants.

Sadly, after sixteen years of marriage, George's wife died at the age of 37. 'She was 11 years younger than me, but in 1970 I married again and we're both still going strong.' Indeed, George is incredibly fit for his age and still goes down to the nursery most days to strike cuttings, pot plants and water them. He did have a spot of arthritis in one wrist and a hand but acupuncture seems to have cured it. That said, George admits to being in semi-retirement, leaving most of the work to some eight staff. 'When I was 82 the accountant said to me, "Now look, you could turn your toes up any time now", so I handed the lot over to my son. I don't drink much and I don't smoke, though I used to as a kid; Woodbines were 2½d for five, but I only ever had 6d so I couldn't get many. Still, I've no plans to retire – not until I go under the daisies.'

At least George will know what people say about him after he has gone. Back in 1983 a lady wrote a letter of condolence to the family, believing that George had died, but it was really his brother who had passed on. He still has the note which includes the passage 'Many many people like myself will miss his cheery face and great personality. The world would be a better place with more persons of his calibre.' There can't be many people who know what others truly think of them, as George now does.

To walk around the nursery with George is to understand his great feeling for plants and the intense pride in his work. Passing from one greenhouse to another, he is bursting with so much energy and enthusiasm that he cannot stop giving a running commentary and constantly pauses to add, 'All these I struck'. Among his favourites are the cedar of Lebanon seedlings which he has taken from the 120ft specimen in his garden. With a girth of 26ft and said to be between 400 and 500 years old, the tree now has many survivors, thanks to George's nimble fingers. Among grateful recipients has been the National Trust property, Uppark, near South Harting, which lost its 250-year-old specimen in the Great Storm of 1987. George was pleased to present the Trust with two four-year-old replacements.

Every plant George strikes is neatly labelled and dated, and it is a tribute to his character that even in his mid-eighties he is concerned about tomorrow, religiously scraping off each plant label so that it can be used several times. Perhaps there is also a hint of the old days here, when times were hard and nothing could be wasted.

Moving to another old building, we come across a dilapidated old chest: 'Dad made this in 1906', George exclaims with pride. And nearby is a jumble of old clay pots. 'Are they any better than the modern plastic ones?' I ask George. 'No', he replies, 'but people like to rummage through them and take a few from time to time'.

Then it's on past an underground coal-boiler. 'Once I opened up and found an old tramp in there. "What do you think you're doing?" I asked. "Havin' a warm one mister", he replied. Yes, we've had all types round here, from gypsies who used to buy strawberries to sell on, to important and famous customers such as actor Alec Guinness. We've only had a handful of old cussers as customers, but even they have their uses as they make us appreciate the good ones.'

Around another corner lies a stack of compost bags. 'Everything's bought in nowadays', George declares. 'In the old days we used to

go out and get all our own leaf mould. And there was a time when I'd only buy British, but just look at me now: even my car's a Volkswagen.'

Then we come to the fence and George peers nostalgically through the netting. 'That's part of the old road there', he points out. 'I can remember the tanks rolling along there hour after hour.'

Then, back in the glass houses, I spot a mousetrap. 'You've got to keep 'em down', George says. 'You can get overrun with mice in no time at all. These little break-back traps are the best. Funny thing, last week I had one caught in two traps at the same time – one had his head, the other his tail. Never seen that before.

'We used to use cheese as a bait, but it comes off easily, so we had to burn it a bit to make it harder and smell better. Now we use bird nuts – they stay on really well. Mind you, those damn slugs seem to be able to eat any bait without springing the trap.'

Further along, George spots a touch of whitefly. 'It's a major problem', he sighs, 'but there's not much you can do about it. There is a parasitic wasp you can get to deal with them, but then you always need a few fly left for the wasps to live on!'

George has had pest problems outdoors too. 'Blackbirds and thrushes are the worst on strawberries and raspberries, but jays are devils on peas and beans, pulling the pods apart. With seedlings we have to watch the chaffinches – as soon as the plants show their noses the finches have 'em out for their seed. But bullfinches are the

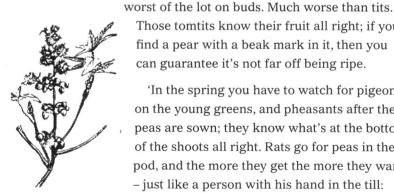

worst of the lot on buds. Much worse than tits. Those tomtits know their fruit all right; if you find a pear with a beak mark in it, then you can guarantee it's not far off being ripe.

'In the spring you have to watch for pigeon on the young greens, and pheasants after the peas are sown; they know what's at the bottom of the shoots all right. Rats go for peas in the pod, and the more they get the more they want – just like a person with his hand in the till:

take half a crown and come back for ten bob. But after a while the culprit makes a clear run and then we know where to set our trap.

'Rabbits always go for the plant that's just been planted and is all droopy with little water. Anyone who keeps rabbits will tell you, they always avoid wet stuff; if they eat it they get liver disease. We all used to keep them to eat. Now the wild ones are really back in numbers. We've got some wallflowers down the bottom and they keep after them.'

Sadly, George died in 1993 and his son subsequently sold the nursery.

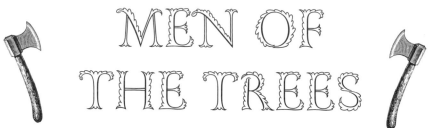

MEN OF THE TREES

Algy and George Lillywhite, Timber Throwers

THERE IS no doubt that tree-felling, or timber throwing, is among the most dangerous of rural occupations, and after a lifetime in the business, brothers Algy and George Lillywhite have the scars to prove it. As soon as you shake hands with Algy you are aware of his missing thumb. 'I was taking. the top out a big ash tree in a farmyard and because of a misunderstanding with the man on the ground a wire slipped and sliced my thumb right off; it could easily have been my arm. That bloody hurt and I thought I was going to faint, so as I climbed down the tree I tried to count all the moths on the bark to take my mind off it. Funny thing is it never really bled.'

On another occasion Algy nearly lost a foot. 'It was first thing in the morning and I took a big swing with the axe, which went straight through the wood – must have been a bit of tension in it – and my boot. All my toes and the front of my foot was hangin' down, but they managed to stitch it all back together again. We was strong in those days, but you 'ad to be to swing an axe all day.

'Chainsaws was really dangerous when they first came in – German Kirchners just before the war. We was about the first to have them. We had the first Danarm Tornadoe in the country, both one- and two-man, with a butterfly chain. One day we were felling an ash when the wind blew the tree back and it whipped round again in a second. The chainsaw took the lace off my left boot and went into my right leg. I had to have 36 stitches, but that night I managed to get down to Goodwood Club.'

George remembers the time they were working on the Goodwood estate when a branch fell out of a tree and hit another man on the back of the neck. 'It must have been stuck up there after being broken off in a storm. Anyway, it part paralysed him. That was the worst accident we ever saw.

'Yes, it's a rough and tumble job all right. I broke my ankle only three years ago, when a tree rolled on it. And Algy has broken three ribs on one occasion and four on another.' Then there was the time when Algy was using a power saw and was thrown 10ft up in the air by a branch which came up between his legs when a tree rolled round. 'It all happened in slow motion really, but fortunately I had the presence of mind to throw the saw away when I was goin' up; no way I wanted to come down again with that in my hand.

'You've really got to be on the look-out all the time. And in the old days back in the sawmill it was common for a man to lose a finger. How there weren't more people killed after the Great Storm of 1987 I don't know. There was yobbos all over the place cuttin' up – and spoilin' timber through splittin' it – without any experience at all.'

Christened Algernon, Algy was born on 12 November 1926, and George was born on 26 October 1928, in a remote cottage in the woods, at Red Copse, near Boxgrove in the parish of East Dean, Sussex. Their father was a gamekeeper on the Goodwood estate. 'But 'e was also very good with his hands and became the village carpenter – makin' threshin' drums, even gunstocks – as well as a gravedigger and welldigger at East Dean. That was after he was made redundant, but they was good to him and sold him a rood [¼ acre] of land on which he built a house. He was one of the men made redundant because there were a lot of death duties to pay when the Duke of Richmond died.

'Grandad had also worked around East Dean, on farms, mainly thatching. We had three sisters and a third brother who was older,

but he was killed when he was 21. He came down the hill just up the road when it was dark and wet and you couldn't see much and ran straight into the back of a horse and cart on his motorbike.'

The boys went to the local school at East Dean and never had any illusions about their future employment. 'With no transport to get out the villages there was no option. It was either Green's sawmill or the farms. But they were enjoyable times and we never went hungry. One thing we do remember, though, is having to go to the isolation hospital at Chichester by horse-drawn ambulance when we had scarlet fever. One boy in the village died of it.

'After father left the duke, he 'ad the rabbit catchin' in return for lookin' after the wild game. In those days there were thousands and thousands of rabbits. Father got 9s a dozen for the largest, 6s for the next size down and 4s 6d for the smallest. In those days you usually bought the right to catch rabbits; you bid off the farmer or he would say a price. It was commonly known that rabbits would pay half the tenant farmer's rent.'

So at the age of 14 George became a full-time rabbit catcher and in his first winter he alone had caught 3,800 rabbits. 'Most were caught in snares but a few were ferreted. In the winter I run about three gross of wires plus gin-traps, but it was always wires in the autumn.

'We made our own entertainment then and we all had guns. There were very few deer but lots of foxes, and we used to catch them as well as badgers and stoats. We used to get penny a pair for starlings' or blackbirds' or any songbird's wings. They were dyed different colours to go on the sides of ladies' hats. But we used to get 6d for a pair of jay's wings, as they're blue and colourful. A weasel fetched 1s 6d, a stoat 2s and a mole 4d or 6d, dependin' on whether it was low or high grade.

'Best of all was badgers, which fetched at least £1 each. To get 'em we used to make our own cartridges up with big lead balls and hide up a tree at night with a shotgun.'

Once George sent off two badger skins to Horace Friend, the dealer, and had a postal order for 30s each back, which was a lot of money then. So Algy thought, 'I'll have some of this and I went up next night to wait for 'em. But I lay on the ground, thinkin' it was all right as long as I got the right way of the wind. Anyway, after a while I heard the badgers come out, rustlin' the leaves in the holes. Then I heard them all around me and I was frightened because I remembered the story of the drain man who put his rods up a den and got attacked. So I jumped up, fired two shots in the air and ran off with nothin'.

'Another thing father and us always used to do', said George, 'was put people's animals down when they wanted it. We used to get 5s or 7s 6d for this, but I always used to make 'em dig their own holes.

'The life seems hard now but we never once thought trappin' was cruel; it was a way of earning a living – survival. And as the war went on everyone was after rabbits and you got as much as 2s 3d for one, but the farmers soon put the price of the ground up. It was only seasonal work – the breeding was more to a set time then and all the rabbits lived in holes whereas so many live up top now. So come March we had to find other work.'

When Algy left school, also at the age of 14, he went timber throwing with his father for £1 a week. 'He did all the hard work and I started off with a 4½lb boy's axe, the heavier ones beinc 6lb and 71b. We'd trim the bottom of a tree down straight and then cut a sink, which gave the direction to throw the tree. It was all piece-work for Green's sawmill at

Chalton, near Singleton. The gang was paid three ha'pence a cube [cubic foot]. Later I went into the mill itself to help father build big sheds.

'After that I joined the gang of hauliers bringing timber into the mill. We 'ad this French lorry which ran off charcoal. It had this big furnace on one side with pipes all over it. You'd start it in the morning with a small amount of petrol and then run for the rest of the day on the gas given off by the charcoal.

'In our youth they still used horses at Goodwood. All the fields was ploughed with horses. The only mechanical thing you saw was a thrashin' machine.

'In the early days we used to bring in trees 80–100ft long. When the two dukes died within seven years there was a lot of death duties and the estate had to sell the whole of Chalton Forest and all the woods to the north. It was estimated over a million cube and at the time was the largest sale of timber ever recorded. Green's bought the lot and it worked out a real bargain – something like a farthing a cube. That was in the early Twenties and how Green's got established in the South. We came in on the throwing side towards the end of the thirty years or so it took to cut the lot down. A great deal of it was sold for Lee-Enfield rifle butts.

'When the war came father was too old to join up and I was "grade 3" – 'ad a weak stomach, but I did go in the Home Guard. And I did see some action. One day I was at the sawmill talking to a manager who was blind and partly deaf. Suddenly Gerry appeared, coming down the valley from nowhere, and the bullets was 'ittin' the ground just 2–3ft behind this manager. Well, I turned and run in the workshop and dived under the bench. Then I thought, "This is no good, he's going to come round again", so I slid under a lorry being

ICE IN WARM CHAMBERS

THERE were some circumstances attending the remarkable frost in January 1776 so singular and striking, that a short detail of them may not be unacceptable. January 7th – snow driving all the day, which was followed by frost, sleet, and some snow, till the 12th, when a prodigious mass overwhelmed all the works of men, drifting over the tops of the gates and filling the hollow lanes. On the 14th the writer was obliged to be much abroad; and thinks he never before or since has encountered such rugged Siberian weather. From the 14th the snow continued to increase, and began to stop the road waggons and coaches, which could no longer keep on their regular stages; and especially on the western roads, where the fall appears to have been deeper than in the south.

On the 27th much snow fell all day, and in the evening the frost became very intense. At South Lambeth, for the four following nights, the thermometer fell to 11, 7, 6, 6; and at Selborne to 7, 6, 10; and on the 31st of January, just before sunrise, with rime on the trees and on the tube of the glass, the quicksilver sunk exactly to zero, being 32 degrees below the freezing point. During these four nights the cold was so penetrating that it occasioned ice in warm chambers and under beds; and in the day the wind was so keen that persons of robust constitutions could scarcely endure to face it. The Thames was at once so frozen over both above and below bridge that crowds ran about on the ice.

WILLIAM HOWITT
Book of the Seasons, 1830

repaired there and in my panic fell into the inspection pit. After a while I realised that the plane had gone and went back out. To my amazement the manager was still there talkin' away, not realisin' that I'd gone. He didn't even know what happened, till I shook him by the shoulder. He was a lucky man.

'The plane didn't do much damage, though one shell smashed all the works of a steam crane on rails, used for lifting timber, and the operator was so frightened he never worked again. A neighbour picked up a shell and burnt her hand on it. Later her husband made a lighter out of it. After, we discovered that the German plane was shot down.

'Sometimes, when we was out rabbit-shootin' we used to have a go at the doodlebugs with our .22 rifles.

'After the war a lot of German beech came in and we went to do piece-work on the bandsaws in the sawmill. But after a year we were like caged animals so we went on our own loggin' firewood. A farmer gave us a wide rood of hedge, but it was full of shrapnel as it had been part of a firing range in the war. It was an awful job to sell firewood in those days. We sold most of ours to a Major Mould from London. Once he gave us a lorry because he said it was unlucky and he couldn't do any business with it. He just left the keys and took the train back to London. But we did all right with it.'

After that the brothers went loading timber for Green's, and left in 1951 to fell timber on the Goodwood estate. In one wood alone, in Singleton Forest, they worked for eight years, under contract to the Duke of Richmond. Most of the trees felled were beech up to about 180 years old and were planted by the second duke. 'Elm was almost a weed in those days, but now it is relatively rare and expensive.'

The Lillywhites have worked in all weathers, even in the great freeze-up of early 1963, 'when the felled trees dropped out of sight in the snow. But there was always some seasonal work to do, such as rinding (taking the bark off), which had to be done just before the buds break and the sap rises. We'd chop a piece off the standin' tree and if it came away clean it was all right. After chopping around the bottom, we'd get the rinding iron in and take a ring off as high as we could comfortably reach. Then the tree would be felled and the rest taken off.

'The bark was put in stacks to dry, then bundled and sent on to the yards for tanning hides. We worked in pairs as part of a gang of eight or ten. Rinding was for about six weeks – all on oak. The bark has to be fresh for tanning to get the acid.

'Summers was spent trimming and taking the cordwood out. A cord is 4ft lengths stacked 2ft high and 16ft long. You need an oppis [Hoppus] book and a special tape for measuring the volume of the trees, but I can more or less do it in me head', says George. 'In winter we'd cut the beech.'

Nowadays the Lillywhites do very little timber throwing, the battle-scarred brothers admitting 'it's a young man's game'. Instead, they concentrate on the sawmill, which they took over about fifteen years ago and stands on part of Green's old site, which itself was on an earlier mill. Here they have the capacity to cut anything up to 32ft long. The biggest piece of wood they ever had to supply was oak measuring 29in square by 17ft long for a windmill, and it had to be very carefully chosen so that it would not crack under stress. Other monsters they've handled include a cedar of Lebanon measuring 8ft across and weighing 23 tons, which had to be felled when its top blew out in a storm. It was sold to Germans for veneer.

UNCONTROLLED FIRES

THOUGH 'to burn on any waste, between Candlemas and Midsummer, any grig, ling, heath and furze, goss or fern, is punishable with whipping and confinement in the house of correction'; yet in this forest, about March and April, according to the dryness of the season, such vast heath-fires are lighted up, that they often get to a masterless head, and, catching the hedges, have sometimes been communicated to the underwoods, woods, and coppices, where great damage has ensued. The plea for these burnings is, that, when the old coat of heath, etc., is consumed, young will sprout up, and afford much tender browse for cattle; but, where there is large old furze, the fire, following the roots, consumes the very ground; so that for hundreds of acres nothing is to be seen but smother and desolation, the whole circuit round looking like the cinders of a volcano; and the soil being quite exhausted, no traces of vegetation are to be found for years. These conflagrations, as they take place usually with a north-east or east wind, much annoy the village with their smoke, and often alarm the country.

GILBERT WHITE
Natural History and Antiquities of Selborne, 1789

The brothers employ two other men at the mill, including one of Algy's sons. Now he, in turn, hears the stories which have been passed down from generation to generation. A favourite goes back many years and was told to Algy by his father, who claimed that it was the most reliable account.

'In the woods above East Dean – almost at the highest point in Sussex – is a large beech called the Sergeant's Tree, which was witness to a sorry tale. In the days of the press-gangs there was a lad called Alan from Heyshott who delivered meat, and his last stop was at the bottom of Bury Hill, where he called in the pub. Inside, two soldiers asked him if he'd like a drink, so he took a pint with them. But as he drained his tankard a coin dropped in his mouth and he put it in his pocket. So the soldiers grabbed him, saying he had taken the King's shilling and had to go in the Army.

'Later the lad deserted and went into hiding. He lived in a boundary bank, which became known as Alan's Bank. His mother and sister used to leave food for him in the crook of a tree and he'd collect it at night. Then he became a highwayman with a musket and was captured on Bury Hill. When he was being chased he shot an Army officer called Sergeant, who fell by a tree. The Duke of Richmond said that tree was never to be cut down and it remains there today.

'The lad ran on to his native Graffham, where he grabbed 'andful of straw from a rick, jumped into the stream and lay in the water under a bank, breathin' through a straw. But eventually the soldiers saw him and shot him in the water. This was way before my father's time, but it's the story as 'e told me.

'One story which was from father's youth concerned some Mormons, who were great con men and baptised some local girls in a dewpond before taking 'em away to America. The local lads was so angry they harnessed the horses to the Mormons' carts the wrong way round – facing the carts – and thrashed 'em. 'Course, a horse will only go forward so they went in the pond and got stuck!'

The brothers were themselves great practical jokers in their younger days. For example, there was the time when they were 11 and, with a pal, rolled a big lorry tyre down the hill. 'It crossed the road, scared a man half to death, buckled the postmaster's bike and ploughed into an old, disused shepherd's hut.'

It is not surprising that these two 'chips-off-the-old-block' are part of a close-knit family for they married two sisters. Their stories of earlier domestic life are legion.

'In the war we used to keep pigs and each year a family was allowed to keep one pig for each bacon ration given up. The biggest porker we had weighed 40 stone and took four men to carry. We used to cure our own bacon, which was normal then. The hams was rubbed with salt every other day for three weeks and then smoked for three weeks. It 'ad to be a sawdust fire of oak and beech, never softwood. One ham we had for seven years.

'But that was nothin' compared to a chunk of venison we kept. Father had this deer which was shot in the front leg and very bloody, so he decided to smoke and cook the leg for the dogs later on. But it obviously got overlooked and was still hangin' up when father died. We saw this thing in the corner all covered in dust and realised what it was. So Mum soaked it in water – it puffed right up again – and cooked it. We all had a little taste and it was perfect, but we decided to give it to the dogs, which is what it was intended for. Only difference was it was 25 years later and not the same dogs! And the meat had only been smoked.

'In the war we used to keep a lot of bees, but not just for the honey. You was given an extra allowance of sugar which you was supposed to feed to the bees, so we never went short of sugar. We used to make our own hives, too.'

Those days of austerity have long passed and the Lillywhites now deservedly live in comfort, in a village which has seen remarkable changes in a relatively short time. Nowadays no one needs to let rooms to visitors to Goodwood races in order to supplement their meagre income, and ham comes from the nearest hypermarket rather than from a pig. kept in the backyard. And where Algy once lived next door in a thatched cottage, he now lives in a modern bungalow on a piece of land sold to him by the duke. Yet the memories remain and the countryside surrounding Charlton is as inviting as ever.

George Lillywhite died in 2000, aged 72,
and Algy died in September 2007, aged 81.

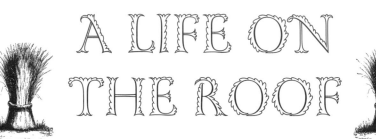

A LIFE ON THE ROOF

Ernest Sharp, Master Thatcher

A TWENTIETH-CENTURY bungalow in suburban Berkshire is not the sort of place where you would expect to find in retirement a man who has spent most of his life perpetuating the chocolate-box image of Old England. But, master thatcher Ernest Edward Sharp has never been one to romanticise about the English countryside. Even at school, he regarded following in grandfather's and father's footsteps as 'just hard work, not something you wanted to do'.

Today this very well-preserved septuagenarian, who retired from the rooftop at the age of 65, presides over a family thatching business which is now in its fifth generation. With his son and grandson now firmly on the rung of thatching success, he is very much the middle man, linking the craftsmen of two centuries through family tradition.

Ernest has always lived in and around the Wokingham area, but it was a much more rural Berkshire when he was born on 22 February 1920. He was one of eight children – six boys and two girls – and remembers getting hay-waggon rides to school, although most of the time they had to walk everywhere. 'You could have walked up the middle of the main road without any fear in those days.'

When he was about seven, Ernest started to help his father with the thatching of hay and corn ricks. 'My brother and I used to harness an old carthorse up and on the cart was a big old water-tank, which we used to take down to the ford at the river and fill the tank up, using a bucket on a rope. Then it was back to the farmyard, where the longstraw was in bundles. It was our job to shake it up with a pitchfork into a bed and every so often throw water over it. Wetting the heap helped to bed it down and soften it. Then we'd start drawing it out by hand into a nice line, the idea being that the wet and weight helped to straighten it out. We drew out bundles 2½ft wide – yelms – then it was onto the rick. Father did the actual thatching and it was the same procedure for rooves.

'Even as kids, we used to spend a lot of time working. During the summer holidays I used to go away with father rick thatching, to Sir Robert Percer's at Colnbrook. We cycled over at first, stayed in a tent and came home at weekends. The work lasted about a month.

'Eventually father got a motorbike and sidecar – a 1,000 twin James – and we was in luxury. But this was nothing compared with his first car. He was doing ricks for the doctor who owned Warfield Park. There was this old Wolsey in the barn and dad asked the doctor what he was doing with it. He said you can have it for £3 10s) and so he did. It was a French-built car and the doctor had collected it from the dock.

JOLLY HARVEST

IT IS IN the wheat-field that all the jollity, and gladness, and picturesqueness of harvest are concentrated. Wheat is more particularly the food of man. Barley affords him a wholesome but much abused potation – the oat is welcome to the homely board of the hardy mountaineer, but wheat is especially and everywhere the 'staff of life'. To reap and gather it in, every creature of the hamlet is assembled. The farmer is in the field, like a rural king amid his people – the labourer, old or young, is there to collect what he has sown with toil, and watched in its growth with pride; the dame has left her wheel and her shady cottage, and, with sleeve-defended arms, scorns to do less than the best of them: – the blooming damsel is there, adding her sunny beauty to that of universal nature; the boy cuts down the stalks which overtop his head; children glean amongst the shocks; and even the unwalkable infant sits propt with sheaves, and plays with the stubble, and with all its twined flowers.

GILBERT WHITE
Natural History and Antiquities of Selborne, 1789

Funny thing is, father drove it home on Saturday and we all went to the seaside in it on the Sunday, even though he'd never driven a car before. I was about ten then.'

Before the days of easy travelling, most countrymen had to be very adaptable to keep themselves in work, and the thatcher was no exception. 'Right up to the war the average thatcher was no businessman, just a tradesman. Most of them regularly had to do other work, especially hedging and ditching in winter and helping with the harvest. There just wasn't the money being spent on house thatching then, but in the 1930s a rick thatcher – provided 'e could do the job right – could earn more than most people.

'And just after the war, too, it was a good living. I used to get £5 for a big rick-some big as a house – and £3 10s for a small one, and as I could do one a day, £25 a week was a mighty good living, a dream for most people. But there was no rush to do it because most people were being lured away into industry in those days. Anyway, it was a good thing that many thatchers packed it in after the war because there were too many of us.'

In April 1940, Ernest volunteered for the Grenadier Guards and, after postings at Chelsea and Windsor, saw service in North Africa and Italy, during which time he was caught up in the horrors of Anzio. Fortunately, he escaped injury, although he did cut his head when he drove his lorry over a cliff. He was in a convoy travelling along a mountain road in Algeria when the lorry in front broke down. 'I stopped, then pulled out to go round him, but we slid over the edge. My mate was asleep but that soon woke him up.'

But Ernest hated the Army and left as soon as he could, in 1946, having married a local girl, Iris, in 1945. So it was back into thatching with father and brother.

One of the more unusual jobs which Ernest used to help his father with was welldigging. 'He did the digging and I used to help lug the clay out with a bucket and rope. The depth varied a lot, according to the water-table. The one in the garden here is just 21ft, but one at Barkham was 100ft. I suppose most are no more than about 20ft deep. They are lined with a single layer of bricks.

THATCHING TODAY

Thatching is far from being a dying trade and in country districts, such as rural Dorset, a considerable number of new homes are built each year with thatched roofs. The basic techniques of constructing and repairing thatch remain the same as they have since Neolithic times, and every trained thatcher will still always place each bundle of reeds so that its thick cut end is the only part visible when the job is finished. The biggest problem faced by today's thatchers is the limited supply of good-quality thatching straw which, for the past 30 years or so, has been grown as a crop in its own right, rather than being a useful by-product of the cereal harvest. As a result, Britain's thatchers are not only importing straw and reed from Turkey, as well as from Poland and other Eastern European countries, but are also experimenting with alternatives including flax, sorghum and miscanthus. The National Association of Master Thatchers (www.nsmtltd.co.uk) promotes all aspects of thatching, including new roofing and thatch repairs, as well as the training of new thatchers.

There remains a big demand for skilled thatchers. The best way to train is to become apprenticed to a master thatcher; to become fully qualified will take up to four years and possibly longer. Thatching training courses are run by several further education colleges, including Hereford College of Technology and Oxford Brookes University, both of which run their courses in partnership with Knuston Hall Thatching School in Northamptonshire (www.knustonhall.org.uk).

'I suppose well-digging can be a bit dangerous, but the worst that ever happened to me was knocking a thumb-nail off when I was breaking up the top of an old well. Mind you, my uncle dropped half a brick on dad's head when he was labouring for him once.'

Like most country folk, the Sharps were fairly self-sufficient, with about 500 chickens and some two dozen milking nanny goats. 'And we used to eat the young billies at six months – lovely meat, absolutely beautiful. I remember during the war being sent with a pony and trap to pick one up for my brother's wedding reception.

'We used to kill the goats by tying a rope round their legs, stringing 'em up and slitting their throats. Grandfather was a pig killer too, and went all over the place. Sometimes I used to help him. The last one I remember was while I was still at school. It was in the dark and I held the torch while two or three men held the pig down and grandad stuck the knife in.'

From those early days, the number of insects about stands out in Ernest's memory, 'especially the dragonflies down by the river'. But insects have caused a few problems in his thatching career, during which he has been stung by wasps on many occasions. 'Once I went to do a little repair job for an ol' feller, and I went to bat up under the eaves. The old devil, he knew that nest was there but never told me. All he did was laugh when I got stung, but a kind woman next door came out and rubbed half an onion all over the swellings. I was ill for a week. In most cases a wasp nest is in the roof space, but this one was in the thatch.'

Unfortunately, Ernest has never found any treasure in a thatch, although his son Geoff recently found a bundle of love letters in one made of Norfolk reed. This is by far the best thatching material and when well laid should last for over eighty years. 'But it's also the most expensive and with all the drainage water reed is increasingly hard to find. Sometimes we have to go over to France to get supplies.

'Longstraw is the cheapest of the three main types. Made from threshed wheat straw of fairly good length, this is the traditional thatch of the South, South East and Midlands. It is recognised by the split hazel rails at the eaves, inset with cross spitting, and when thatched by us can last up to 30 years.

'Devon reed – combed wheat straw – originated in the Westcountry, but has spread over the Home Counties, is recognised by its smooth mushroom-shaped thatch, and has a lifespan of up to forty years. The Norfolk reed is found mainly in East Anglia and the Home Counties and gives a smooth thatch with angular lines.

'Costwise you are talking thousands for a complete new thatch, but it might be ten or it might be 20; the price varies enormously according to the size and the number of complications as well as the type of material used.'

Now Ernest proudly relates that his son has re-thatched some longstraw work he did over 35 years ago, 20-30 years being the average for this cheapest of thatches. His son has even thatched in France, but generally they stay within Hampshire, Gloucestershire, Surrey, Oxfordshire, Berkshire and Buckinghamshire. He has never been tempted to move to an area with more thatch 'because there are certain to be more thatchers there. It's got so much more competitive over the last ten years. Everyone thinks it's a goldmine, but nobody wants to work the five- or six-year apprenticeship there used to be.'

Apart from the family trio, the Sharp business employs four other men, 'and there was a time when my wife Iris used to labour for me too. But she could only do ground work because she didn't like coming down the ladder. And it's best if everyone in the team works at about the same pace. Mind you, I'm a bit of a rusher, always wanting to get the job done. But I suppose it's been a business for me. Those old boys certainly worked longer hours than the men today, but then they were only plodders.'

Despite all his rushing, Ernest has survived to tell the tale, although he has fallen off the roof quite a few times. Once when he was working at Ascot he was up and down a ladder all day before it broke and he fell some 15ft, but he got away with only a broken ankle. And on 1 August, 1985 (he remembers the exact date because they were due to go on holiday that night) he broke an ankle when he jumped down off the straw on a pick-up truck. His foot twisted when he landed on a ball of straw. So instead of going on holiday he began a seven-month lay-off.

A more serious accident happened in his early 30s when he was cutting holly. 'The holly was in great demand for wreaths and crosses and we used to make hundreds of 'em. But it was mother's trade really and we used to take them to Brentford Market. Anyway, this particular year I stepped on a dead branch when moving between trees, and fell 20ft straight down. Somehow I managed to drive the motorbike and sidecar home and when the doctor came the next morning he told me I'd broken two vertebrae. I ended up in plaster for four months.'

But despite smoking from the age of 22 until he was 68 ('I used to roll my own'), Ernest never set a thatch afire. 'Of course, I never smoked on a job. But I do remember when a steam-engine went through and set a thatch ablaze.'

During his long career, Ernest has worked for many distinguished people, Berkshire being a renowned haunt of the rich and famous, close enough to London but with a generous sprinkling of old cottages. Among his clientele have been Tiny Rowlands, King Hussein (at Windsor), the Sultan of Oman, actress Beryl Reed ('do call me Beryl') at Wraysbury, Hollywood actress Jacqueline Bissett, and even the Queen, for whom he re-thatched the princesses' play-house at Windsor.

Apart from houses, Ernest has thatched all sorts of buildings, from the barn at Eton College to a school at Hartley Wintney in Hampshire. 'Sadly, it was knocked down years ago.' He even thatches new buildings – 'We've done four in the last year'. And sometimes he is asked to make animals and birds from thatch. 'One American got me to make two thatched pheasants for him to take back and put on his shingled roof!'

Fortunately, the thatch does not have many natural enemies, 'though rats and squirrels will chew holes in it. It's not our fault, though, but where the owners are not aware they have pests in the building. You can thatch a roof well and go by soon after and see where rats have punched holes in the wire-netting, from the inside. It seems incredible that the owners don't know they are there. Oh, and then there's bloody magpies, which I've known to pull out long reeds for no apparent reason. They simply kept returning to the same spot in the thatch, pulled out the water reed and dropped it on the ground.'

But these have been minor problems in what has been a generally successful thatching career. 'You didn't get a lot out of life much of the time, but we had a lot less hassle than many people.' And years of running up and down ladders obviously still left Ernest with enough energy for recreation, as his main hobby has been cycling. Before the war this involved time trials, but with the arrival of Continental refugees road racing started. 'In the old days, under National Cycling Union rules, no bare legs were allowed, so we wore black tights and an alpaca jacket. It was nothing to go 50 miles, but it was immensely enjoyable then as there was so little motor traffic.'

All this activity has certainly left Ernest with a sparkle in his eye, which is just as well as he believes that 'any thatcher must have a good eye for lining things up. And the other essential quality is a head for heights; you never hold a ladder, always working with both hands.' But as well as his trade skills, Ernest always had a good business sense, unlike 'some of the best thatchers I knew, who didn't earn any money. Trouble was they didn't know when they'd done it good enough.' And it is this ability to combine quality craftsmanship with business acumen which has enabled the Sharps to survive in the profession for over a century.

Ernest Sharp died in 2001, aged 81. His son has also since died and the business is now run by Ernest's grandson, Scott.

MAN OF IRON

George Ranger, Farrier

IT SEEMS odd that a man who has spent over 50 years shoeing horses has never ridden one, but it is no more surprising than the fact that for much of that time he has successfully operated from his home on a town council estate. Of course, the days have long gone when the clip-clopping of horses was an everyday sound about our streets, so George James Alfred Ranger became one of those great survivors who ply their trade from the boot of a car. And on his wide journeying afield, from Godalming in Surrey, he has acquired a knowledge of animals that is second to none.

Born at Newhaven on 30 November 1924, George was the son of a chauffeur gardener and the grandson of a farm labourer. The family moved to Godalming in 1927, when the old Surrey town was a great centre of rusticity far removed from the commuter stop fast-train travellers know today. Nonetheless, the surrounding countryside remains sufficiently unspoilt to provide George with enough work for the remainder of his days, and shoeing horses is what he plans to do until the day he drops.

With 'big brother' Guildford nearby, even in the Twenties communications were relatively good in the area, so when the Ranger family went walking, as they often did then, it was easy to get a bus back. They never kept horses – 'just a dog and a few chickens'.

While still at Busbridge School, George and his brother collected sackfuls of leaves and sold them to keen gardeners for a penny a barrow. But at that time he had no special aspirations and certainly never imagined that he would become a farrier.

'In those days jobs was few and far between so it was a question of get what you could.' So, like so many of his contemporaries, when he left school at 14, George took a local position as a garden boy. 'There were three of us in Sir Fred and Lady Radcliffe's garden, and for working from 7am till 5pm Monday to Friday, but 12 pm on Saturday, I had 5s a week. Mother took half.

'For the next two years I was expected to do everything – especially weeding and hoeing. One of the head gardener's favourite tricks was to get me weeding the crazy paving on a cold February morning; then my fingers were nearly dropping off.'

At the age of 16, George learned about a job at the local forge through his brother. When George told Sir Fred that he was leaving his employment, his boss offered to increase his wages to 10s a week. However, he wanted a job with more of a future and proceeded to join 66-year-old Frank Brown at the Shackstead Lane forge, even though his starting wage was only 5 s a week.

THE FARRIER TODAY

For over 3,000 years farriers have been shoeing horses – and this means of keeping horses' hooves sound continues today. The Farrier Training Agency (www.farrierytraining. co.uk) is the body that oversees the training of new recruits to this ancient profession and apprenticeships can be applied for through them. As well as skill with metal and forging, a love of horses is essential to success. The Farriers Registration Council www.farrier-reg. gov.uk is the statutory body for farriers, concerned with the welfare of horses as well as with training farriers in correct and humane practice.

The modern blacksmith has come a long way from the farm gate. As well as shoeing horses, many craftsmen produce both beautifully made useful objects ranging from gates and railings to shoe scrapers and umbrella stands but also pieces that are pure works of art including jewellery and garden statues. Thanks to a resurgence of interest in the craft of metalwork of all kinds there are now more blacksmiths working today than there were 30 years ago. Equally, smiths are expanding their craft to work with other metals such as copper and bronze and incorporating materials such as wood and stone into their work. More information, including details of courses, can be found at www.artist-blacksmith.org.

George did not undertake a formal apprenticeship with indentures, but in Frank Brown he had an excellent teacher, the old master having practised at the forge since 1915, following an apprenticeship with local firm James Luck. Brown truly loved his work and had been shoeing a horse only a few days before he died at the age of 82.

Fortunately for George, he was not called up when war broke out. Besides the fact that he was deaf in one ear, farriers were in demand for shoeing the Army mules. In fact, his was a relatively peaceful war; the closest he came to seeing action was when he watched a German bomber crew – 'I could see their faces' – who flew low over Godalming to drop their load. 'But only a few windows were broken.'

It was during the war, on a visit to his sister at Newhaven, that George met and married Lily.

When George started at the forge in 1941, the tractor revolution was not underway, so there were many farm horses to shoe. But horses were also used for road transport – 14 for Stovold's Dairy, three for the Co-op and one for the bakery. 'I particularly liked the baker bringing his old horse up because he used to bring me fresh cream buns and lardy cakes so greasy you haven't been able to get the likes of 'em for years.' The dairy ponies were the first horses George ever handled.

Most villages had a farrier then, including nearby Milford, Compton, Famcombe and Eashing. Godalming still had two farriers, but the town had five up until the early 1920s.

But George's work was never entirely devoted to horses. At the old forge they always did general blacksmithing, including ornamental ironwork such as gates. George was also a very good wheelwright and they made entire wheels, not just the metal 'tyres'. Another popular line was their wheelbarrows, which were completely hand-made from wood and iron for just 70s.

The old brick forge had been converted from two cottages. One half contained the main forge and workbench and the bottom half was devoted to shoeing.

'By golly, it was hot in there, especially when we had a big wood fire going for the tyres. Those cartwheel tyres needed a huge blaze. It was very heavy work and needed several of us working quickly together. Smaller tyres were made whole and knocked firmly onto the wood before cooling and shrinking, when they were nailed into place.

'But the bigger tyres had to be made in sections and were nailed separately to the wheel. The biggest we ever made were loft high and went on a timber cart at Busbridge Hall. It was used for hauling great trunks out the forest. The wheel stocks were elm, and the spokes and felloes (circular bits) ash. We last made wheels in the 1950s.

'In very dry weather tyres sometimes had to be taken off and a piece of metal taken out because they had shrunk and become loose. To avoid this some old boys used to wrap wet sacks around the wheels when they were not in use.'

In those early days, when local communities had to be more independent and every hard-earned penny had to be accounted for, farriers such as George were called upon to be 'horse doctors'. For example, if a septic spot was encountered while shoeing a horse it made sense to cut it out there and then. In the vast majority of cases this was straightforward, the customer was happy because more often than not he was not charged anything for the extra service, and George gained a little goodwill for his business. But inevitably, with

ENTERPRISING SWALLOWS

WE HAVE known a swallow build down the shaft of an old well, through which chalk had been formerly drawn up for the purpose of manure; but in general with us this hirundine breeds in chimneys; and loves to haunt those stacks where there is a constant fire, no doubt for the sake of warmth. Not that it can subsist in the immediate shaft where there is a fire; but prefers one adjoining to that of the kitchen, and disregards the perpetual smoke of that funnel, as I have often observed with some degree of wonder. Wonderful is the address which this adroit bird shows all day long in ascending and descending with security through so narrow a pass. When hovering over the mouth of the funnel, the vibrations of her wings acting on the confined air occasion a rumbling like thunder.

A certain swallow built for two years together on the handles of a pair of garden shears, that were stuck up against the boards in an outhouse, and therefore must have her nest spoiled whenever that implement was wanted: and, what is stranger still, another bird of the same species built its nest on the wings and body of an owl that happened by accident to hang dead and dry from the rafters of a barn. This owl, with the nest on its wings, and with the eggs in the nest, was bought as a curiosity worthy of the most elegant private museum. The owner, struck with the oddity of the sight, furnished the bringer with a large shell, or conch, desiring him to fix it just where the owl hung: the person did as he was ordered, and the following year a pair, probably the same pair, built their nest in the conch, and laid their eggs.

GILBERT WHITE
Natural History and Antiquities of Selborne, 1789

development of animal welfare and jealous guarding of veterinary practice, such work is now a thing of the past. Since the Farriers Registration Act, 1975-77, you even have to be a registered shoeing smith to shoe your own horse.

Putting the shoes on is only part of the work. Trimming the feet, which grow continually like fingernails, is necessary too, for goats, cows and bulls as well as horses. 'And trimming an ol' bull is no joke either, as their owners know. I always remember General Molyneux at Loseley Farm getting me out there under false pretences to do a horse, but I coped with his bull all right. These great big animals are a bit different from the mini donkeys at Crystal Palace and Battersea Park children's zoos, where I have been going for some years.'

When it was still common to see work horses on the road, many animals were brought to the forge for attention, but even in the early 1940s George had to go out to some on the farms. 'And this was no mean feat on a push-bike, laden down with two sets of cart horse shoes weighing 16 lb, not to mention all my tools, including hammer, pincers, rasp, tongs and buffer. This was all cold shoeing, of course, the animals having already been seen and their shoes shaped pretty accurately back at the forge.' So it was a marvellous day when George first acquired a car.

In 1941 a set of shoes cost about 7s 6d, but nowadays George charges from £30, his prices being very competitive – 'one cowboy charges £69 for a simple set'. Overcharging is even less excusable

TRAPPED TITMICE

THE BLUE titmouse, or nun, is a great frequenter of houses, and a T, general devourer. Besides insects, it is very fond of flesh; for it frequently picks bones on dunghills: it is a vast admirer of suet, and haunts butchers' shops. When a boy, I have known twenty in a morning caught with snap mouse-traps, baited with tallow or suet. It will also pick holes in apples left on the ground, and be well entertained with the seeds on the head of a sun-flower. The blue, marsh, and great titmice will, in very severe weather, carry away barley and oat straws from the sides of ricks.

GILBERT WHITE
Natural History and Antiquities of Selborne, 1789

today when the bulk of shoes come ready-made, supplied by specialist factories. All the farrier has to do is order the closest size, heat the shoe up and knock into precise shape. Special shoes are usually made in consultation with a vet.

'Even bars of shoe iron come ready-grooved now, whereas we used to start with 12-16ft lengths of straight iron and had to put the groove in ourselves. Racers, of course, generally have aluminium plates. As the old trainers used to say, "an ounce on the foot is worth a pound on the back".

'On average, a horse wants shoeing every six weeks, even if the shoes aren't worn, because the feet need trimming. But there are individuals among horses just as there are among humans, some nails growing quicker than others and some shoes wearing quickly. One of Stovold's old dairy horses needed new shoes every four days, but then the trouble was there were so many nail holes it was a job to find space for new ones. And it is important that the nails only go up the wall of the hoof as the centre part over the sensitive area is surprisingly thin.

'At the other extreme, one pony I used to do only needed shoes every two years. And when the feet are trimmed it is perfectly all right to put the same shoes back on if they are not worn.'

Although farriery suffered a major setback with the widespread use of tractors after the war, the great upsurge of interest in leisure riding more than compensated. Previously, it was generally only the wealthy who rode for pleasure, but now, with an ever-widening network of pony clubs and riding stables, there is a good future for farriery, as long as adequate training is provided. Furthermore, George has had steady work with polo and show ponies in summer and hunters in the winter.

But even with the advent of mechanisation, a surprisingly large number of work horses lingered on. Some villages still used a horse and cart to empty toilet buckets for many years after the war, and a few very traditional farmers clung to their plough horses up to the early 1970s. For example, 'old Mr Secret kept his on because he believed that the tractors hardened the soil too much deep down'.

There was a wonderful partnership between the ploughman and his horses; he knew that to get the best from them they had to be treated with kindness and understanding. Consequently, they would be worked in teams and they all had a couple of months off each year, on a rota. It was George's job to take their shoes off before they were turned out in the fields.

George did not start with an innate love of horses, but he has acquired great respect for them. And, as Lily Ranger emphasises, 'he's got an awful lot of patience'. He is convinced that they have a fair degree of intelligence, too. 'One little Shetland I used to shoe would often pull my braces as far as he could and then let them go with an almighty thwack just for the fun of it.' And there is no denying the fun they have given George: 'I used to wear a beret which became so nibbled it looked like a colander'.

However, George has had his fair share of accidents, too, having been burnt, bitten and kicked on many occasions. His worst burn happened when he slipped and the welding torch seared the back of his hand. The scar on his upper arm is a reminder of the day when he was bitten by a mare with a foal, whose feet he was trimming while it was held by its lady owner.

Some ten years ago he was knocked unconscious by a kick on the side of his head. 'I have no idea what happened, but when I woke up there was a lady standing over me with a wet towel and a glass of whisky. She took me to the house, where I had two more Scotches before driving home. Apart from a headache, all I suffered was a black eye.'

According to George, the way to avoid being kicked is to work 'as close to the animal as possible'. But there are bound to be times when the unexpected happens, for example when 'one old shire had both feet over my shoulders – a very lucky escape for me'. Then there was the time when he was tapping a shoe-nail in, the horse flinched and the nail went into his arm.

George has always used coal for his forge – 'you can get a much greater heat than with gas. Also gas does not produce a big enough hot area for larger items such as the S-shaped wall retainers.'

The boot of George's car is just big enough to take his mobile forge, anvil, block and tools, but only if they are packed in precise order, which he does without thinking, having done it a thousand times before. But there was at least one occasion when his generally meticulous routine failed. After a shoeing, the powdery coal must be extinguished with water so that the forge can be put back into the car. But one day George did not put it out properly and as he motored along black smoke suddenly started to billow from the boot. Fortunately, the customer he had just left was one of many who constantly supply him with flasks of coffee and on this occasion the beverage was sufficient to douse the unwanted fire.

But it is not just coffee that George has been given by grateful customers, some of whom he has been visiting almost since the day he started. In 1991 friends and clients put on a surprise party for him in recognition of his 50 years in the business. And what a variety of clients he has had, ranging from a 95-year-old with two active hunters to a little girl who said: 'Why aren't you miserable like all the other blacksmiths?'; from nobility and high-ranking officers with strings of polo ponies to celebrities such as Tubby Turner of television's Ermmerdale Farm.

Yet George would never pretend that his clientele is one big happy family. Indeed, there have been many thoughtless or selfish people in his life, especially those who ring up late in the evening and expect a pony to be shod for a show the next morning. In fact, George often attends shows as duty farrier, ready to replace shoes which, for example, have been kicked off in horse boxes on the way to the events.

George has certainly not made a fortune from farriery and neither has it left him fighting fit. On the contrary, he now walks with a pronounced stoop after all those back-breaking years. 'But I'm lucky because I'm not very tall; a lot of taller ones end up with serious back trouble.' He also emphasises that great strength is not a prerequisite for farriery: 'It's your way with animals that counts'.

Apart from working closely with animals, George has found wrought-iron work most rewarding, and now many of his pieces adorn the houses of friends and relatives, including that of his daughter. She, too, has a keen interest in horses, and this in turn has rubbed off on George's grandson whom he would like to see follow him at the forge. But he will have a long wait because George insists that 'I won't give up horses until they give me up'.

George did not fully retire till 2008, at the age of 84.

KEEPING THE HOME FIRES BURNING

Wally Joyce, Chimney-sweep

THE DENSE woods which cloak the hills around Haslemere conceal much more than a wealth of wildlife; here, too, is an exceptional richness of old buildings. And where the dwellings of past centuries persist, so too do open fires. So what better a place could a chimney-sweep hope for than this pot-pourri of Old England, where the corners of Surrey and Sussex curve gently around each other? Here, in this living museum of architecture, where black-beamed cottages jostle with tile-hung terraces, Georgian mansions and modem mayhem, are stacks and flues of every shape and size, and no one knows their inner secrets better than Walter Charles Joyce.

POOR WAYFARERS

OF ALL THE vast class of human creatures who are doomed to diurnal weariness – to know the bitterness of the labour that is done under the sun – there are none that I can more feelingly sympathise with than the daily wayfarers; especially in the season of shortening days, frequent storms, and growing cold. I do not mean the wealthy, the lazy, and luxurious viatores that, in carriage, or on steed, traverse the king's highways, in great bodily comfort, and, after a few hours' career, alight in elegant homes or wellgarnished inns, and stretching themselves at their ease, with every requisite of viand, wine and feather-bed at command, but I mean all those who, being of the poor, are never to cease from the land; and whom, whether we be seated at our tables, circling our fires in social mirth, or quietly laid in our beds, we may be sure are scattered in a thousand places on our great roads, be it summer or winter, day or night, as plodding, as full of trouble, as weary, and as picturesque as ever.

WILLIAM HOWITT
Book of the Seasons, 1830

Now 65, Wally Joyce continues the business established by his father in 1934. Wally took it over in 1964, when his father died of lung cancer. Whether Joyce senior's death was anything to do with his occupation we do not know, but he was a heavy smoker.

Wally was born on 24 April 1927, just outside Haslemere, at Hammer, where his grandfather worked in the brickworks. Ironically, one of the first jobs Wally's father did was to help to take down the chimney stack at the brickworks.

CHIMNEY SAFETY TODAY

Providing quality, safety and good service are the aims of Britain's prime organisations for chimney sweeps, including the Institute of Chimney Sweeps (www.instituteofchimneysweeps.co.uk) and the Guild of Master Sweeps (www.guild-of-master-sweeps.co.uk). As well as being the source of soot and even potentially dangerous gases such as carbon monoxide, unswept chimneys are a common cause of household fires, which can be highly dangerous to both life and property. Courses for chimney sweep training are provided by both bodies, and qualified sweeps will become familiar with all types of fire, flue and chimney, from the historic home to the new-build and from the Aga to the gas burner. As well as the traditional brushes, most modern chimney sweeps use specially adapted vacuum cleaners to suck up flue debris and reduce the risk of soot fall and damage to a minimum. For the biggest chimneys, industrial vacuum cleaners adapted with filters to cope with the debris are used.

In those days Haslemere was a very sleepy country town, and with unspoilt countryside pressing down on all sides, especially around Hammer, the area provided the ideal environment for a lad to grow up in. But for the labouring classes there were few opportunities to break away, so few eyebrows were raised when Wally left school at 14 to become a garden boy earning 30s a week.

But Wally was disillusioned by his work for Mr Muir, at Rowallan in Haslemere. 'They kept pigs, goats, ponies and rabbits, and I seemed to spend all my time looking after them rather than gardening. One of the other gardeners used to cut bracken for the animals' bedding, and I helped him rick thatching, too. It was all done with scythes.

So young Joyce soon moved on to become a gardener at Great Stoatley, Haslemere, the home of the appropriately named Mr Greenacre.

By now World War II was well underway and rationing had a significant impact on most aspects of life. But the enterprising young Joyce soon found a way round the shortage of mowing petrol. 'The trick was to start the old Dennis with only the carburettor full of petrol; when it was warm it would run for the rest of the day on paraffin.'

At 16 to 18 years old, Wally was in the Air Training Corp (ATC) and went on an air frames course, but there were no vacancies in the Fleet Air

Arm so he was called up into the Army. He went to the Athens area with the East Surreys, but saw only twenty-eight days' war service.

When Wally left the forces he thought that gardening would be a poor living, so he went to work for his father. 'I joined two other men he employed then and did mostly window cleaning.' At the time there were many more sweeps in the area. Nowadays, however, sweeps are 'a scarce race', as Wally puts it. 'Although round here there is no smokeless zone and open fires remain popular, overall the "box" (TV) has become the focus of a room and many houses do not have a single fireplace.'

Working within about a 7-mile radius around Haslemere, Wally and his father began travelling around on a motorbike and sidecar. Their first van was a three-wheeler Reliant, and there followed a succession of plain vans. Wally has never been attracted by gimmicks such as having a chimney and brush protruding from the roof of his van, and he does not even have his name painted on the side. 'Fortunately, I don't need to advertise, and in any case a plain van is easier to sell.'

Sometimes he travels further afield when a good customer moves away and does not want to lose Wally's very reliable service. He even managed to do his round on the morning after the Great Storm of 16 October 1987, when hundreds of mature trees blocked most of the roads in the area. 'I had to drive under great branches arching over the lanes in many places and none of the customers expected to see me at all.'

Not surprisingly, it was after the 1987 storm that Wally noticed how many more jackdaws began to nest in chimneys and flues. This engaging little member of the crow family has always been keen on

COTTAGERS FARE

COTTAGERS now [March] gather the tender-springing tops of nettles to make pottage, considered by them a great purifier of the blood. They also boil them instead of spinage, as they do the tops of the wild hop, as a substitute for asparagus. But of all the vegetables that are cultivated, next to the potato, rhubarb has become, perhaps, the most valuable to the poor, and pleasant to all. Of late its growth has rapidly increased; and people who, some years ago, never saw such an article exposed in our markets, are now astonished at the quantities brought there, and disposed of with the greatest readiness. As a most wholesome and agreeable vegetable, coming in early and supplying a delightful acidulous material for pies and puddings, till gooseberries are ready, it is invaluable, and seems destined to acquire universal estimation.

WILLIAM HOWITT
Book of the Seasons, 1830

chimney nest-sites, but tree holes have also been used extensively. Sadly, so many of the old trees which harboured suitable hollows were blown down in 1987, compounding extensive losses through Dutch elm disease.

'Jackdaws have always been a big problem in the area. Once, at the Old Rectory, by the Black Fox at Milland, I took ten jackdaw nests out of 12 chimneys, and afterwards I had enough sticks for Bonfire Night. And on another occasion I dragged down a brood of young jays in a jackdaw nest.'

Squirrels, too, can be a problem. 'Once, down tumbled four pink babies among the sticks blocking a chimney. Other times they can be the stinkiest thing going, when you pull one down which is decomposing and all maggoty. And get them in your roof and you can be in for a real mess. But the one I remember most was shriekin' and squealin' like a mad thing; I must have caught her in a soft bit with my nest hook and she shot out the chimney at 90mph and dropped 20ft into a tree.

'Then you get the bees, and dragging them down is no joke.' But Wally has not had any serious accident caused by wildlife. Human error has been much more significant: he attributes his exceptionally bushy eyebrows to frequent singeing. Once he was almost roasted alive in the boiler-house at a Guildford hospital. 'The boiler man was getting impatient as his pressure was dropping, and he didn't realise that I was still working on the flue. Fortunately I had stepped back when he opened up and the roar just missed me.'

There are many inglenooks and large stacks on his patch, but Wally has never actually been stuck in a chimney. However, on several occasions he has had to call for help when trying to reach a flue. For example, there was the time at the Manor Hotel, Hindhead, when he had to crawl under the floorboards to reach a soot door. His bulky overalls held him firmly so he had to wait for someone to come and pull him out.

Another time he was making a regular visit to Holly Ridge, the Surrey County Council children's home. 'I had to lay in an awkward position across the top of the boiler to empty the back flue. But they never told me that the plumber had just been in to fix extra pipes. Again, my overalls pinned me down and I had to shout for the gardener to pull me out by the legs.'

Apart from boiler flues and standard chimney-stacks, Wally also cleans some old kitchen ranges and many Agas, which have become increasingly popular as part of the nostalgic movement towards creating times past.

But there is not much romance in chimney-sweeping. Wally generally works at least a ten-hour day, from 8am to 6pm, or often much later in the winter darkness. 'In the old days we always started at 6am, but nowadays we have the problem of catching people in, as so many wives go out to work.'

Some of the buildings which Wally visits belong to the rich or the famous, ranging from Lord Tennyson's poetic pile high up on Blackdown to comedian Terry Scott's modern bungalow. A few are exceptionally eerie, too, including the one-time base of Oliver Cromwell, where Wally had to stay very late cleaning no less than 26 chimneys; working alone, he was unnerved by the atmosphere.

Nowadays, few people are interested in the soot collected from the chimneys, but there was a time when Wally and his father would sell it all to keen gardeners. Indeed, when Wally himself used to work as a gardener he would take some soot in a hessian sack to his employer's garden, where it was put in a water butt for feeding the tomatoes.

'Soot was also put on onion beds, and we used to mix it with lime to make a paste for dipping cabbage or sprout plants in to combat club root. A ring of soot around a plant would keep the slugs off, and one old gardener I knew used to brush it on the lawn with a birch broom as it lay on the broad-bladed weeds and killed them but did not harm the narrow grass. Nowadays we give the soot to customers. And another thing, soot is really good for rose-beds; it must be, because in industrial areas you never used to get black spot.'

Wally has never used a vacuum – 'You have to sweep the chimney anyway. Some of the older people still cover absolutely everything up when they know you are coming, but others are so unprepared you even have to take the hot ashes out the grate. But I am pleased to say that my reputation has been a clean sweep and there is no doubt that your reputation travels with you.'

Some customers are surprisingly unhelpful. 'For example, at one house I struggled for over an hour before I discovered that the chimney. Then there are the DIY people who call you in without telling you what they have done. Many's the brush I've dragged out of a chimney. With a difficult flue you musn't keep bashing away hoping to find a way up, but patiently twist around with the brush.' And you cannot carry too many 3ft rods – Wally needs no less than 26 for tackling the flue in one building converted to flats.

The Joyce household itself does have an open fireplace, but Wally admits that they rarely use it. 'We have Calor gas in the living-room and I've got one of the dirtiest chimneys in Haslemere; my boiler chimney only gets swept when soot falls down and puts the fire out. No profit in it, is there?' Today Wally charges about £14 to sweep an average chimney, whereas in 1964 it was 7s 6d. But there is no doubting that he provides value for money, because he is booked up weeks ahead and still has some of his father's customers.

When Wally knocks on your door on a dark winter's evening, after a long day grovelling in grime, all you can see is the whites of his eyes flickering beneath his cap, and you wonder if his tough skin will ever be clean again. Yet he is in constant demand for one of those ceremonies when everyone must be whiter than white, the wedding. 'It's usually the bride's mother who invites me, because she believes that it is good luck if the sweep is the first person the bride sees when she comes out the church. So, I have to turn up in my overalls, complete with rod and brush, and get to peck the bride on the cheek as well as shake the groom by the hand. It's one of the perks of the job.'

As you watch Wally at work, bent over the hearth staring into a black hole, you may feel that he needs many highlights to brighten his week. But remember, for every hour he spends surrounded by soot, he has another travelling around some of the most beautiful countryside in southern England.

Wally Joyce is now enjoying his retirement.

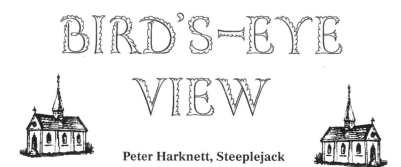

BIRD'S-EYE VIEW

Peter Harknett, Steeplejack

F EW PEOPLE have had such a good view of the changing rural
scene as that enjoyed by Peter Harknett. Not only has he spent
his entire working life on the tops of tall buildings – mostly country
churches – but also he has travelled the length and breadth of the
land. But sadly, his bird's-eye view of Britain, spanning a lifetime
at the top, has made him realise just how much of the countryside
has been lost. 'There's far too many cars and people now, and I'm
very worried about the amount of building going on.' And when,
like Peter, you return to a place perhaps decades later, you really do
appreciate the piecemeal destruction of our green and pleasant land.

But Peter's pinnacles of achievement have not only been in this country. His highest job has been at the 900ft level on the 1,000ft-high Eiffel Tower: 'We were doing maintenance and painting and you couldn't see Paris for the drizzle'. And he has worked on domes in Israel and the Arab countries. 'But as a Jew, in the old days I needed two passports! Nowadays it's a lot easier.' He even tried to straighten the Leaning Tower of Pisa: 'I wrote with suggestions on how to shore it up, but I never got the job'.

At home he has worked on some impressive buildings, too, including the National Gallery and the Houses of Parliament: 'I gilded the crowns on the Commons and 400ft above London was a very interesting place to be'. But no place was more inspiring than the spire of St Mary's Battersea, 'where they say Turner used to paint'. In fact, he has maintained and surveyed many important buildings and monuments, not to mention industrial premises and follies, but his heart is firmly in the country. 'It's amazing how many village churches there are tucked away – I still hear of new ones even now.'

Now devoted to his adopted Sussex, Peter Ronald Harknett was born in Marylebone, London on 4 December 1934. His interest in and willingness to accept heights is easy to explain: his grandfather worked on rigging in the Navy, including on the Royal Yacht, 'and father did rigging too, before going on to tall buildings and churches. He carried on active work into his late 1960s, but when he died in 1990 no one knew how old he was. He must have been gone 90, so hopefully I've got a long way to go yet.'

When World War II broke out, Peter's father was exempt from call-up as he was needed to work on dangerous buildings following air raids. The Blitz also meant that young Peter and his brother had to be evacuated to Cornwall, near Redruth. 'And that was a-bit of a problem because we were Jewish and one of the first things we were given was a plate of pork sausages. But then we just had to get on with it, and I've been the same since. I'm very interested in Judaism, but not to the extent I won't have a bacon sandwich if I fancy one.'

Despite continuing hostilities, the boys returned to London to finish their schooling – 'I never did know why mother took us back while the war was still on'. While he was still at school, Peter started to help his father with steeplejacking, and at the age of 15 went to work full-time. 'Sons always looked up to their fathers in those days' – literally, in Peter's case.

'In the 1940s there were lots of great big chimneys in London and I was never afraid of going up. But as the son I got all the menial tasks and the odd cuff round the ear. I was mostly looking after ropes – father was a very fussy man and liked everything put away properly. We never really got on. But even if there was nothing to do I liked to climb up just to have a good look around. Then, as now, we'd always start about 7.30 in the morning and work till dark. I always work a six-day week, and often seven, as do my two men. I really look forward to going to work. When the weather's nice and you're up there 12 hours a day it can't be beat; the only thing is at my age I'm starting to feel the cold a bit. The satisfaction is fantastic and the job so variable, working on lead, copper, stone, wood and gilding. You're not a master craftsman, but you learn bits of many trades. You don't do the carving or whatever, but you must know how to put it in place properly. I would say it's a craft and you become a jack of all trades.'

STEEPLEJACKS TODAY

As for the steeplejacks of old, a good head for heights, physical fitness and a willingness to work outdoors in all weathers remains an absolute essential for anyone contemplating work on tall buildings, bridges and towers as a 21st century occupation. Yet for trained steeplejacks, who in Britain number some 1,000, there is plenty of work – whether repairing, painting, demolition or rebuilding. And today's steeplejack has the benefit of safer specialist scaffolding and so-called fall-arrest devices, which significantly reduce the risk of accidents. To become a steeplejack the best way to train is through one of the apprenticeship programmes set up by the steeplejack industry. Before being accepted, applicants are asked to take aptitude tests and are carefully assessed for their ability to work at heights. The website www. atlastraininggroup.org.uk/apprentices.php includes details of how to begin the training process.

Not surprisingly, Peter is frequently asked about the dangers of the job, but he insists that 'it's the safest job in the building industry. I've had a couple of minor falls but never a serious accident. You see, you put the rigging up yourself and because you are aware of the height you make sure you do it properly. It's not like in the rest of the building trade, where one man puts up the scaffolding, another man comes along and moves a bit then a third one falls off it. We know our own rigging and make sure it's right.

'Sometimes the young ones start showing off a bit, swinging around when the girls walk by – it's only natural; but if they do, I come down on them like a ton of bricks. The life insurance is not loaded at all, but the employer's liability is crippling, even though there are few claims.

MUD BUILDINGS WE HAVE NONE

THE VILLAGE of Selbourne, and large hamlet of Oakhanger, with the single farms, and many scattered houses along the verge of the forest, contain upwards of six hundred and seventy inhabitants. We abound with poor; many of whom are sober and industrious, and live comfortably in good stone or brick cottages, which are glazed, and have chambers above stairs: mud buildings we have none. Besides the employment from husbandry, the men work in hop gardens, of which we have many; and fell and bark timber. In the spring and summer the women weed the corn; and enjoy a second harvest in September by hop-picking. Formerly in the dead months they availed themselves greatly by spinning wool, for making of barragons, a genteel corded stuff, much in vogue at that time for summer wear. The inhabitants enjoy a good share of health and longevity: and the parish swarms with children. It appears that a child born and bred in this parish has an equal chance to live above forty years. Chances for life in men and women appear to be equal.

WILLIAM HOWITT
Book of the Seasons, 1830

'I did once fall 40ft, but nothing bad happened to me. The worst fall we had was when one of the men was 85ft up and his ladder came back, so he fell 64ft onto a church roof, smashing through the slates and timbers. He was unconscious and at first we thought he was dead, but next morning he was fine, having suffered only two broken ribs and a disclocated finger. The unfortunate thing was that on the morning of the accident the vicar had asked me to be finished by 2pm as a wedding was due, but when the bride arrived the ambulance and fire brigade were still trying to get the injured man out – most embarrassing. And it cost me £500 to repair the roof!

'The funniest thing that ever happened to us was when a priest asked me why a non-Catholic wanted to work on his church and he seemed very concerned about the insurance. I told him not to worry because the building was well covered, but he was more concerned about us. When I first started going up the tower he could not bear even to look at me, but as the days went by he got braver and started to watch. Eventually, on the last day, he plucked up courage to wave as he walked by, but at the same time tripped over and broke his leg! Then we had to wait ages till he came out of hospital before we got our money.

'I should think the most dangerous job we've ever done was at Hadlow Castle in Kent. The top blew over in 1987 and it was very tricky indeed lowering the pinnacle down. But then I've always done this sort of work and think nothing of it.'

Ironically, storms have provided some of the materials for Peter's work, in the form of timber to make the shingles (wooden tiles) which are now in such great demand for church spire restoration. He is a keen conservationist and will not hear of a tree being felled specially to provide shingles.

'Most of these Sussex churches were designed for oak shingles and now there is a great movement to put them back as they were, which is surprising really as this must be the most expensive roofing in the world, at about £70 a square yard for the materials alone. And the stainless steel nails cost about £1,000 on the average spire. The nails used to be copper, but even those were attacked by the acid in the wood till the heads dropped off. We also make chestnut shingles and apparently they last as long as oak, but you can't tell them apart when they're old. Mostly we work in oak – there's so much of it around here. We've used a lot of trees from the Great Storm, so there's no waste; I like it that way.

'Traditional shingles should last 100 years. I've taken off a lot that age, but with our nails they could be up a lot longer. These new nails are one modern thing I'm all for.'

Sadly, all wooden materials have their natural enemies, 'mostly deathwatch and furniture beetles. And there's a big problem with woodpeckers, too. At Lynch, in Sussex, we were asked to put a cedar roof on and just three years later we had to do it again, in hardwood. The green woodpeckers had ruined it. And at Sandhurst one went right through a shingle while we were having a cup of coffee. It's the insects they're after – they can hear them. We treat the outside of the spire but that only lasts for a year or so. You need these insecticide smoke-bombs let off inside regularly: they're really good. Usually, when you strip off a spire you have insects by the million. I have a beardful every night and have to comb it out. The only answer where there's a serious woodpecker problem is to change the covering – it's very much in areas.'

Woodpeckers are not the only birds which Peter encounters in his high life. 'I met a nice kestrel on Chichester Cathedral spire once.

We came face to face, looked at each other a few moments and then off he flew. And once when we went to work at Ewhurst Church, in Surrey, there were about 50 pairs of swifts nesting there, so we had to go back. We did what we could, but of course they can't get in there any more.

'Nowadays, any time we come across bats we have to stop work immediately and notify the authorities to get permission to continue. They're fully protected now and rightly so. Once we found a roof at Worcester absolutely alive with bats – they were all around the laths when we took the tiles off. Some fell out and we tried to put them back as best we could, but you always lose a few through shock.'

Sadly, Peter has to leave a spire birdproof, so many traditional nest-sites are being lost. 'At Farringdon, Hampshire, we had to take out three young barn owls before sealing up, but the local publican reared them, only losing one. We always find someone to take them in.' How sad that few buildings do not retain their special owl windows, which used to be so common, although there is concerted effort by the Hawk and Owl Trust to encourage their use.

On another occasion, at Preston Candover, in Hampshire, 'the sticks were 26ft deep in the tower of a Victorian church where the jackdaws had nested for so long. We had to clear the lot out, but didn't find any jewellery like they're supposed to collect, only plenty of silver paper and bottle-tops. And do you know, the birds tried to peck their way back in for a week or so, so we had to redo the lead; then they gave up. You mustn't leave any opening.

'A very creepy experience with birds happened at Porthleven, in Cornwall, when we were working on the spire along the harbour wall. For some reason, the seagulls there were a real nuisance and almost attacked us. It was especially unnerving as we'd only recently seen Alfred Hitchcock's horror film *The Birds*.'

After completing each major job, Peter likes to leave a record for future generations, so he prepares an airtight lead envelope which he fixes inside the spire. He puts general comments along with some of the photographs which he always takes from the top of the spire or other vantage point. 'I like to think that my spire will last for a century or two and when some future steeplejack comes back he can see the way it used to be. I also leave my own thoughts on the people I have had to deal with.'

Peter certainly never gets bored when he is working. 'I'm a great thinker and there's always some problem to overcome. Take Guildford Cathedral, for example: we've had a contract to look after it for over 20 years and I'm always having to come up with ways to stop the water coming in. One of the things I do is think to myself in Hebrew, and I also read and write in Hebrew.'

But being so conspicuous in his work, Peter inevitably gets into conversation with passers-by, which sometimes causes confusion. 'When we put up a weather-vane we always do it with the aid of a compass, but you always get some local coming along who insists that north is in a different place.'

Peter clearly does not suffer fools gladly, and for that reason alone you are compelled to believe him when he tells you that he has seen a ghost or two, the most memorable of which was in Kent.

'When we go away on a long job we mostly take our caravans and put up in the churchyard. On one occasion we were at Boughton under Blean – a 'plague church' outside the town – and where an ol' boy told us some Jews were buried. Anyway, I had to go to get our water through the churchyard, and when I did one evening a chap walked right past me down the path. I didn't think too much of it at first, but next day I realised that I had been able to see him clearly with my light switched off.

'Next night I saw him again and he was wearing Jewish clothing. I spoke to him but he didn't reply and disappeared into the night. Later, local people told me that the path on which he walked didn't go anywhere and was now a dead end.

'Some time after that I was working in Sussex, not too far away, and decided to run over to Boughton to take another look. As I parked the car I happened to notice the time on the dashboard. I went into the churchyard and the ghost came out from behind a grave carrying a menorah [seven-branched Jewish candlestick]. Again he ignored me and walked right past. And when I got back into the car I was astonished to see that I had been gone an hour when it seemed like minutes.' For a man close to God in more ways than one, it was a moving experience.

Kent remains one of Peter's favourite counties, but for him Sussex will always be his first love. Yet he will go where the work is, even though he has never needed to advertise his services. There are some 40 firms – mostly family businesses employing four or five men – in the National Federation of Steeplejacks & Lightning Conductor Engineers and their motto is: 'Any height, anywhere', which is supposed to reduce competition.

Sadly, Peter believes that he will be the last of the steeplejack Harknetts. 'My stepson is a lecturer working abroad and my brother couldn't even stand on a table. It's a shame. Young steeplejacks have always liked the travel – new town, new girl, but of course it never happened!' That may be so, but there is no denying that Peter has had his fair share of adventure and has certainly seen the high life. His view of the British countryside has been remarkably revealing.

In 2010 Peter was still going strong at the age of 75, as the oldest working steeplejack in Britain.

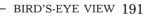

Stan Thorne, Stickmaker

NOWADAYS THERE are amateur and even semi-professional stickmakers in every county, tucked away in outbuildings and garden sheds, working with the hazel, holly and other woods taken from local hedgerows and copses. Many make more sticks than they need and give them to friends or perhaps sell a few at country shows. But few could contemplate the vast numbers which have passed through Stan Thorne's hands, for he spent over 50 years working for one of the oldest-established walking-stick factories. But it was a very different business when Stan started out.

INVITING FOOTPATHS

I LOVE our real old English footpaths. I love those rustic and picturesque stiles opening their pleasant escapes from frequented places and dusty highways into the solitudes of Nature. It is delightful to catch a glimpse of one on the old village-green; under the old elder-tree by some ancient cottage, or half hidden by the overhanging boughs of a wood. I love to see the smooth, dry track, winding away in easy curves, along some green slope to the church-yard — to the forest grange — or to the embowered cottage. It is to me an object of certain inspiration.

WILLIAM HOWITT
Book of the Seasons, 1830

The grandson and great-grandson of chairmakers at High Wycombe, in Buckinghamshire, Stanley Ralph Thorne was born in London on 26 January 1927. His father was a freelance stick bender and one of the companies he worked for was Cooper's of Wormley, Surrey, for whom he worked full-time from 1938. Thus Stan was destined to grow up as a country boy, truly living 'in the sticks', for all around them were the plantations from which the factory took some of their wood.

The family moved into a company cottage at Chiddingfold, next to the stable for the company's horse and cart, which took the finished sticks to the local railway station at Witley. 'In those days they more or less grew walking-sticks. Small ash plants were bought-in from Belgium, cut back to one eye and planted on their side with the eye sticking up. They grew from the eye and after five or six years were dug up, the roots cleaned off to form the handle and the stem the shaft. While they grew a man went round to take off all the leaves and shoots. Now there is a council estate where those ash plantations grew.'

Large quantities of ash, hazel and chestnut were bought by the acre from neighbouring farmers or landowners, and cut by gangs of Cooper's own men between September and March, the tops being used to make 'pimps' or faggots for firelighting. Indeed, this was especially convenient, for the village of Chiddingfold has long had one of the most celebrated bonfires in the country, and traditionally Cooper's used to supply two lorry-loads of faggots to dress the bonfire on Guy Fawkes Night. Now the faggots are not available, but up till 1991 the company still supplied the sticks for the many torches used in the street procession.

When he left school, at the age of 14, Stan worked for six months with the butchers, Furlonger's of Chiddingfold, for whom he had worked part-time while he was at school. 'It was not very pleasant work; they killed their own cattle on the premises and for £1 a week I had to do a bit of everything, including scraping the hairs off the pigs after they had been scalded in hot water. But I got out and about a bit, delivering their meat and home-made sausages on my bike.'

Then it was into Cooper's 'factory', which was then merely a collection of buildings added piecemeal after Henry Cooper established the firm in 1850. Stan became one of about 50 employees who worked from 7.30am to 5pm, 5½ days a week for 25s. 'I was supposed to do the usual bender's seven-year apprenticeship, but did two and went in the Navy for three years. I was only 16 when

MAKE YOUR OWN WALKING STICK

Making your own walking sticks – and creating them to give as gifts for family and friends – is a highly rewarding craft. As of old, selecting the best stick is vital, but even if it has a twist in the middle it is essential that it aligns properly at top and bottom. The more knots and marks on the stick the more attractive it will be, but it is important to make sure that any knots will not weaken the finished stick and that it is free of insect infestation that could lessen its durability. A good way of testing the strength of a stick you have cut is to place one end into the trunk of the tree then press as hard as possible on the other. It should bend only a little.

Detailed instructions for making a stick from start to finish can be found at websites such as http://walking.about.com/od/hikingandwalkingsticks. If you are not fortunate enough to be able to obtain a stick from a countryside maker such as Stan Thorne, it is possible to buy kits from companies such as Allgoodideas (www.allgoodideas.co.uk) which also offer a wide range of items to give a handmade stick a finishing touch such as brass and silver collars and handles of all kinds, including duck and horse-head shapes.

I joined up – you should have been 17 – and I became a wireless operator on small coastal craft – torpedo boats, etc. Later I got a government grant under the interrupted apprenticeships scheme. The factory stayed open during the war and had a big contract'to make chestnut ski-poles for the Army.

'First thing in the morning I had to get all the fires going before dad got there at 8 am. I used wood chips – all the offcuts from the making of sticks – and we had to heat the sand for the bending. It was all indoor work and the workshops were very tiny and hot with dirt floors. We only had one brick building then, the rest were wood – shacks really, added as the company expanded. It was very tough then. You either did your job or you were out on your ear; we all had sticks thrown at us. The pressure was always on because after the apprenticeship it was all piece-work and you only got paid for what you done. There was no holiday pay.

'Much of the seven-year apprenticeship was getting to know the characteristics of the many different hardwoods used then for the fancy London trade, including pimento (allspice), kingwood, snakewood, rosewood – that's not what it was then – and ebony. Father and me were two of only three benders in the country who could work well with such hardwoods and cane. I loved the smell of the different woods getting hot and singeing and could identify them all by the smell alone. I also used to bend a lot of cow horn, and once even bent a bit of rhino horn for the boss to put a shaft on.

'In my day we bent completely freehand. The wood was warmed up in the sand, then a gas jet used to give precise heat. You had to know each wood well as some have a very short grain and would snap easily with the wrong treatment. You needed a lot of heat. You started off with a square-shaped piece of wood, bound it with wire and soaked it first. Each night the bent sticks would be stood in hot sand to bake off in position. In the morning we'd tap them and if the string dropped off we knew they were cooked enough. Steam replaced the hot sand in about 1946, when a new bending shop was built, and most of the bending was done by machine in later years.

'The trade has always been about 90 per cent chestnut and ash walking-sticks and in 1991 we turned out about 2,000-2,500 a day, many going to hospitals. The cane trade is more or less finished in this country as the sticks and umbrellas can be brought in cheaper from abroad. We were still making about 2,000 or 3,000 shepherds' crooks a year in the late 1980s, most of them going to Australia and New Zealand.

'We used to make a lot of horse measures. These were hollow sticks with a metal measure, in hands, inside, but they went out in the 1950s, when all the horses disappeared from the land. We also used to make the wooden part for sword sticks, but these were stopped in the 1960s, when people became concerned about offensive weapons.

'A small number of blackthorn shillelaghs [Irish cudgels] were still made in 1991, but nothing like we used to do. By now I think every American must have one on his mantelpiece.' Other casualties of changing times have included manila canes used by headmasters to deal with naughty boys, and the crooked 'Harry Lauder' sticks once the backbone of music hall. And not since the 1950s has Cooper's supplied hazel and chestnut hoops to the makers of dry casks. Yet other special lines continued into the 1990s, including white sticks for the blind, staves and flagpoles for the Scouts and swagger sticks for sergeant-majors and the Zambian police. Altogether, in 1991 the workshop was producing some 600,000 sticks a year and there were 120 employees. Sadly, the company ceased the stick production side of the business in December 1991, finding it cheaper to buy them in from Germany, but Stan Thorne still presides as production manager and can still remember when 'there were enough walking-stick workers from just one family to make up a football team'.

Stan and his wife, who has also worked at the factory, now live so close to Cooper's, in a quiet country lane, that he can hear the factory hooter and it is difficult for him to get away from his work. And with the company's expansion into orthopaedic equipment for the National Health Service there has been considerable local friction. Henry Cooper's original 35 workshops were too inefficient

to run a large business in the 1990s, so the company had to seek permission to develop the site into a high-tech complex. This was granted in 1991, but only after villagers objected to the intensification of an industrial development in a rural area. As Stan would agree, we cannot

TROUBLESOME FLIES

THERE is an insect with us, especially on chalky districts, which is very troublesome and teasing all the latter end of summer, getting in people's skins, especially those of women and children, and raising tumours which itch intolerably. This animal (which we call an harvest-bug) is very minute, scarce discernible to the naked eye; of a bright scarlet colour, and of the genus of Acarus. They are to be met with in gardens on kidney beans, or any legumens; but prevail only in the hot months of summer.

There is a small long shining fly in these parts very troublesome to the housewife, by getting into the chimneys, and laying its eggs in the bacon while it is drying: these eggs produce maggots called jumpers, which, harbouring in the gammons and best parts of the hogs, eat down to the bone, and make great waste. It is to be seen in the summer in the farm kitchens on the bacon-racks and about the mantelpieces, and on the ceilings.

The insect that infects turnips and many crops in the garden is an animal that wants to be better known. The country people here call it the turnip-fly and black dolphin. In very hot summers they abound to an amazing degree, and, as you walk in a field or in a garden, make a pattering like rain, by jumping on the leaves of the turnips or cabbages.

GILBERT WHITE
Natural History and Antiquities of Selborne, 1789

preserve every bit of the countryside as a museum; there always has been change and there always will be. In fact, much of the countryside has suffered since the bulk of the workforce has moved off the land into urban environments and in recent years many villages have become little more than dormitories. It is good to know that in recent years all of Cooper's employees have lived within a 5-mile radius of the Victorian buildings. Countrymen such as Stan Thorne are helping to bridge that gap between the old and the new. Few people have seen such great changes and he is to be applauded for sticking with it.

Stan retired in 1996 and in 2010 was continuing to enjoy his retirement, aged 83.

EPILOGUE

TRUE VALUES

So these have been the long centuries,
   and always what went before was better
in eyes which no new icon could please.
   Our countryman has lived by the letter
of the law of the wild and now sees
   only sadness as the green ways wither
and silence deepens among the trees.

Yet this need not be so.

Surely there is room in every blackness
for a field where the blackbird sings for ever
and man can work in harmony
with all the wild things he has loved.

BRIAN P MARTIN, 1992

ACKNOWLEDGEMENTS

My special thanks go to the 13 men who are the main subjects of this book, for so generously giving of their time and divulging so many personal facts and opinions. I would also like to thank the late Gordon Beningfield, Richard Pailthorpe, the National Farmers' Union at Midhurst, Stephen Lance, Steve Walpalmer of Shillinglee Bee Farm; Ian Odin, head forester of West Dean Estate, Sussex; Sue Hall, my editor at David & Charles; and my wife Carol, for her invaluable help and encouragement.

ABOUT THE AUTHOR

Brian P. Martin has written 25 books on the countryside and natural history, including the best-selling *Tales of the Old Gamekeepers* and six others in David & Charles's *Tales* series, *The Great Shoots* and the international award-winning *Sporting Birds of the British Isles*. Formerly a hospital administrator and commissioning editor of *Shooting Times*, he has written for numerous publications, his *Rusticus* column having run for over 25 years. Born on the Hampshire coast, he has lived in the South-West Surrey countryside for over 30 years.

INDEX